Praise for

"The list of editors is a who's who of American poetry. Above all, the poet David Lehman, the series editor, has labored quietly and diligently ensuring its continuity and continued relevance.... Every year will have its new-discovered gems, its duds, its stars, and, often enough, its brief but vitriolic controversies played out across social media. You might think such a long-running series would have played out its initial energies, but I think I can say with some confidence that Mary Jo Salter's 2024 volume is the best volume in a decade, and arguably the best *BAP* volume ever produced."
—A. E. Stallings, Oxford University Professor of Poetry

"Each year, a vivid snapshot of what a distinguished poet finds exciting, fresh, and memorable: and over the years, as good a comprehensive overview of contemporary poetry as there can be."
—Robert Pinsky

"*The Best American Poetry* series has become one of the mainstays of the poetry publication world. For each volume, a guest editor is enlisted to cull the collective output of large and small literary journals published that year to select seventy-five of the year's 'best' poems. The guest editor is also asked to write an introduction to the collection, and the anthologies would be indispensable for these essays alone; combined with [David] Lehman's 'state-of-poetry' forewords and the guest editors' introductions, these anthologies seem to capture the zeitgeist of the current attitudes in American poetry."
—Academy of American Poets

"A high volume of poetic greatness... In all of these volumes... there is brilliance, there is innovation, there are surprises."
—*Publishers Weekly* (starred review)

"A year's worth of the very best!"
—*People*

"A preponderance of intelligent, straightforward poems."
—*Booklist*

"A 'best' anthology that really lives up to its title."
—*Chicago Tribune*

"An essential purchase."
—*The Washington Post*

"For the small community of American poets, *The Best American Poetry* is the *Michelin Guide*, the *Reader's Digest*, and the Prix Goncourt."
—*L'Observateur*

OTHER VOLUMES IN THIS SERIES

John Ashbery, editor, *The Best American Poetry 1988*
Donald Hall, editor, *The Best American Poetry 1989*
Jorie Graham, editor, *The Best American Poetry 1990*
Mark Strand, editor, *The Best American Poetry 1991*
Charles Simic, editor, *The Best American Poetry 1992*
Louise Glück, editor, *The Best American Poetry 1993*
A. R. Ammons, editor, *The Best American Poetry 1994*
Richard Howard, editor, *The Best American Poetry 1995*
Adrienne Rich, editor, *The Best American Poetry 1996*
James Tate, editor, *The Best American Poetry 1997*
Harold Bloom, editor, *The Best of the Best American Poetry 1988–1997*
John Hollander, editor, *The Best American Poetry 1998*
Robert Bly, editor, *The Best American Poetry 1999*
Rita Dove, editor, *The Best American Poetry 2000*
Robert Hass, editor, *The Best American Poetry 2001*
Robert Creeley, editor, *The Best American Poetry 2002*
Yusef Komunyakaa, editor, *The Best American Poetry 2003*
Lyn Hejinian, editor, *The Best American Poetry 2004*
Paul Muldoon, editor, *The Best American Poetry 2005*
Billy Collins, editor, *The Best American Poetry 2006*

Heather McHugh, editor, *The Best American Poetry 2007*
Charles Wright, editor, *The Best American Poetry 2008*
David Wagoner, editor, *The Best American Poetry 2009*
Amy Gerstler, editor, *The Best American Poetry 2010*
Kevin Young, editor, *The Best American Poetry 2011*
Mark Doty, editor, *The Best American Poetry 2012*
Robert Pinsky, editor, *The Best of the Best American Poetry: 25th Anniversary Edition*
Denise Duhamel, editor, *The Best American Poetry 2013*
Terrance Hayes, editor, *The Best American Poetry 2014*
Sherman Alexie, editor, *The Best American Poetry 2015*
Edward Hirsch, editor, *The Best American Poetry 2016*
Natasha Trethewey, editor, *The Best American Poetry 2017*
Dana Gioia, editor, *The Best American Poetry 2018*
Major Jackson, editor, *The Best American Poetry 2019*
Paisley Rekdal, editor, *The Best American Poetry 2020*
Tracy K. Smith, editor, *The Best American Poetry 2021*
Matthew Zapruder, editor, *The Best American Poetry 2022*
Elaine Equi, editor, *The Best American Poetry 2023*
Mary Jo Salter, editor, *The Best American Poetry 2024*

THE
BEST
AMERICAN
POETRY
2025

◊ ◊ ◊

Terence Winch, Editor

David Lehman, Series Editor

SCRIBNER POETRY
NEW YORK   AMSTERDAM/ANTWERP   LONDON
TORONTO   SYDNEY/MELBOURNE   NEW DELHI

Scribner Poetry
An Imprint of Simon & Schuster, LLC
1230 Avenue of the Americas
New York, NY 10020

For more than 100 years, Simon & Schuster has championed authors and the stories they create. By respecting the copyright of an author's intellectual property, you enable Simon & Schuster and the author to continue publishing exceptional books for years to come. We thank you for supporting the author's copyright by purchasing an authorized edition of this book.

No amount of this book may be reproduced or stored in any format, nor may it be uploaded to any website, database, language-learning model, or other repository, retrieval, or artificial intelligence system without express permission. All rights reserved. Inquiries may be directed to Simon & Schuster, 1230 Avenue of the Americas, New York, NY 10020 or permissions@simonandschuster.com.

This book is a work of fiction. Any references to historical events, real people, or real places are used fictitiously. Other names, characters, places, and events are products of the author's imagination, and any resemblance to actual events or places or persons, living or dead, is entirely coincidental.

Copyright © 2025 by David Lehman
Foreword copyright © 2025 by David Lehman
Introduction copyright © 2025 by Terence Winch

All rights reserved, including the right to reproduce this book or portions thereof in any form whatsoever. For information, address Scribner Subsidiary Rights Department, 1230 Avenue of the Americas, New York, NY 10020.

First Scribner Poetry edition September 2025

SCRIBNER POETRY and design are trademarks of Simon & Schuster, LLC

Simon & Schuster strongly believes in freedom of expression and stands against censorship in all its forms. For more information, visit BooksBelong.com.

For information about special discounts for bulk purchases, please contact Simon & Schuster Special Sales at 1-866-506-1949 or business@simonandschuster.com.

The Simon & Schuster Speakers Bureau can bring authors to your live event. For more information or to book an event, contact the Simon & Schuster Speakers Bureau at 1-866-248-3049 or visit our website at www.simonspeakers.com.

Manufactured in the United States of America

1 3 5 7 9 10 8 6 4 2

Library of Congress Control Number: 88644281

ISBN 978-1-6680-8058-0
ISBN 978-1-6680-8059-7 (pbk)
ISBN 978-1-6680-8060-3 (ebook)

CONTENTS

Foreword by David Lehman	xiii
Introduction by Terence Winch	xix
Gbenga Adesina, "The People's History of 1998"	1
Hussain Ahmed, "Incantation for a Lake"	3
Indran Amirthanayagam, "At the Gate"	5
Margaret Atwood, "Tell Me Something Good"	6
Catherine Barnett, "Nicholson Baker and I"	8
David Beaudouin, "Annunciation"	12
Donald Berger, "Uncle Sadness"	13
Camille Carter, "Thoughts about Inheritance"	16
Grace Cavalieri, "White Suit"	18
Christopher Chambers, "What About This"	20
Dorothy Chan, "Triple Sonnet for Nomi Malone"	21
Heather Christle, "Aubade"	23
Lor Clincy, "Wishes for Black Women"	25
Andrea Cohen, "Fable"	27
Billy Collins, "Thought a Rarity on Paper"	28
Katie Condon, "Book Blurb in the American Style"	30
Morri Creech, "A Letter from Rome"	31
Patricia Davis-Muffett, "Climate Anxiety"	34
Armen Davoudian, "The Ring"	36
Greg Delanty, "To Our Indolent Cancer"	39
Abigail Dembo, "The Travelers"	40
Jose Hernandez Diaz, "My Kafka Prose Poem"	41
Tishani Doshi, "Egrets, While War"	42
Denise Duhamel, "Poem in Which This Fathead 'Fat Ass' Admits It"	43

Elaine Equi, "Lorca's Guitar" — 44
Gerald Fleming, "Two Thousand" — 45
Joanna Fuhrman, "How to Change the Filter on the Developing Cell Matter in Your Womb" — 46
Amy Gerstler, "Postcard" — 48
James Allen Hall, "Inheritance at Corresponding Periods of Life, at Corresponding Seasons of the Year, as Limited by Sex" — 49
Jeffrey Harrison, "Amnesia" — 51
Robert Hass, "A Sunset" — 53
Bob Hicok, "The call to worship" — 57
Nazifa Islam, "The Wind Whipped Tears into My Eyes" — 58
Henry Israeli, "Escape Artists" — 59
Fatima Jafar, "In the End of the Beginning of Our Lives," — 60
Brionne Janae, "The Heart" — 61
Raphael Jenkins, "Two men too man to mourn" — 62
Virginia Konchan, "Miraculous" — 64
Victoria Kornick, "Eileen" — 66
Marianne Kunkel, "Apostate Abecedarian" — 68
Michael Lally, "DC 1972" — 69
Danusha Laméris, "Second Sight" — 71
Hailey Leithauser, "Five Postcards" — 72
Amit Majmudar, "Patronage" — 73
Chris Mason, "Well Water" — 74
Greg McBride, "Know Thyself" — 75
Jill McDonough, "What We Are For" — 76
Joyelle McSweeney, "Death Styles 5/6/2021: *Terminator 2*, Late Style" — 77
Ange Mlinko, "The Bougainvillea Line" — 80
Nicholas Montemarano, "A Neighborly Day in This Beautywood" — 82
Yehoshua November, "What About the Here and Now?" — 83
Sharon Olds, "Health-Food Panties" — 88
Michael Ondaatje, "November" — 89
Pádraig Ó Tuama, "Do You Believe in God?" — 91
Jose Padua, "Godzilla Meets the Beast" — 93

Elise Paschen, "After *Killers of the Flower Moon*" — 94
Alison Pelegrin, "Zero Bothers Given" — 96
Donald Platt, "Streak" — 98
Jana Prikryl, "The Channel" — 101
Elizabeth Robinson, "The Extinct World" — 105
Matthew Rohrer, "Nature Poem about Flowers" — 107
Margaret Ross, "Cooperative" — 110
Javier Sandoval, "Uncle Peyote" — 114
Emily Schulten, "Nocturnal" — 116
Jane Shore, "I Am Sick of Reading Poems about Paintings by Vermeer" — 118
Martha Silano, "When I Learn Catastrophically" — 120
Bruce Snider, "Trio" — 122
Mosab Abu Toha, "Two Watches" — 126
Tony Towle, "Birthdays" — 127
Cindy Tran, "Blank Verse" — 129
David Trinidad, "Never Argue with the Movies" — 132
Bernard Welt, "The Story So Far" — 134
Lesley Wheeler, "Sex Talk" — 137
Geoffrey Young, "The How and When of It" — 139
Kevin Young, "Snapdragon" — 140

Contributors' Notes and Comments — 143

Magazines Where the Poems Were First Published — 185

Acknowledgments — 189

DAVID LEHMAN was born in New York City. A graduate of Stuyvesant High School and Columbia University, he spent two years at Clare College, Cambridge, as a Kellett Fellow. Upon his return to New York, he worked as Lionel Trilling's research assistant and earned his PhD at Columbia with a thesis on prose poems. He taught for four years at Hamilton College, and then, after a postdoctoral fellowship at Cornell, he turned to writing as a full-time occupation. Lehman launched *The Best American Poetry* series in 1988. He edited *The Oxford Book of American Poetry* (2006). *The Morning Line* (University of Pittsburgh Press, 2021) is the most recent of his poetry collections; his prose books include *The Mysterious Romance of Murder* (Cornell University Press, 2022), *One Hundred Autobiographies: A Memoir* (Cornell, 2019), and *Signs of the Times: Deconstruction and the Fall of Paul de Man* (Simon & Schuster, 1991). In 2010 he received the Deems Taylor Award from the American Society of Composers, Authors, and Publishers (ASCAP) for *A Fine Romance: Jewish Songwriters, American Songs* (Schocken, 2009). Lehman lives in New York City and in Ithaca, New York.

FOREWORD

by David Lehman

◊ ◊ ◊

Emily Wilson, whose translations of the *Iliad* and the *Odyssey* have met with wide acclaim, was asked whether she sees herself "as an advocate for classical studies." Her answer: "I know it sounds really earnest and worthy to say it, but yes, I want to be an advocate or ambassador—for Homer, for poetry, for translation, and for ancient literature."[1] I feel the same way about poetry, American poetry in particular, though I am anything but a born diplomat and, as Wilson rightly says, it sometimes feels "limiting to be treated not as an individual artist but as a representative of this larger thing, Poetry."

A poet is not a natural anthologist, for the pursuit of a poetic vision entirely your own clashes with the aim of a collection embracing work by writers associated with as many regions, movements, tribes, and poetic strategies as you will find in the United States. It's not an easy task, but it's an important one if you agree with Joseph Brodsky that American poetry at its best is "a nonstop sermon of human autonomy, of individualism, self-reliance," and that the "grandstanding" he finds in European poetry is "alien to the generous spirit of American poetry."[2] Brodsky felt that every hotel room in the United States should contain, in addition to a telephone directory and a Gideon Bible, a poetry anthology, and perhaps it is a parable that hotel rooms today are devoid of all three of these books.

---

1. Robert Long Foreman and Stefanie Wortman, "A Conversation with Emily Wilson," *The Missouri Review* (Summer 2024):181.
2. Grace Cavalieri, "The Generous Spirit of American Poetry: An Interview with Joseph Brodsky," *Beltway Poetry Quarterly* 10, no. 4 (Fall 2009), https://www.beltwaypoetry.com/brodsky-interview/.

Is there something quixotic about our venture? Undoubtedly. If the editors do their job well, few readers will admire all the poems equally. That is part of the plan. There are, after all, many who disagree with my belief that it is possible to like, say, John Ashbery as well as Philip Larkin, Charles Bukowski, and Adrienne Rich. Any attempt to convey "the generous spirit of American poetry" will prove to be, as has been said of psychoanalysis, not only impossible but also very difficult. How do we solve the problem? We don't, but we do our best, and as the poems in each year's *Best American Poetry* are chosen by a different guest editor, the series as a whole, now numbering thirty-eight volumes, represents a bold and significant effort to lessen the difficulty.[3]

Terence Winch, who chose the poems for this volume, has all the qualities one seeks in an editor: He has excellent, wide-ranging taste and is generous but discriminating—and very smart. For *The Best American Poetry 2025*, Terence has chosen poems of wit and whimsy, memory and premonition, deep feeling and profound meditation. The book contains sonnets, a sestina, an abecedarius, and a villanelle; poems that rhyme and poems that don't; prose poems, discursive meditations, a free-verse aubade, a fable, a "People's History of 1998," and a "Poem in Which This Fathead 'Fat Ass' Admits It."

The subjects that engage our poets include Franz Kafka, Godzilla, birthdays, sex, "health-food panties," amnesia, Houdini, the movies, ancient Rome, and a "shoebox full of peyote buttons." Pádraig Ó Tuama asks an old question that has perhaps recovered its pertinence: "Do you believe in God?" Robert Hass's poem "A Sunset" foregrounds the tension many poets feel between the freedom of the aesthetic imagination and the imperatives of moral judgment. It is difficult to imagine a poem with a more stunning opening than Martha Silano's offering. The poem's title: "When I Learn Catastrophically." The first line: "is an anagram of *amyotrophic lateral sclerosis*."

It came as no surprise that Terence displayed an exemplary dedication to the project. I have admired his poems and stories for many

---

3. There are forty volumes in the series if we include the two retrospective collections, the "best of the best" books edited by Harold Bloom (1998) and Robert Pinsky (2013).

years and have also witnessed his remarkable ability as an editor. Since the summer of 2020, he has edited the "Pick of the Week" feature on *The Best American Poetry Blog*, and it has deservedly gained an ardent following. Each week Terence matches a poem he admires with visuals beyond the usual: a work of art that exists in stunning counterpoint to that week's poetic "pick."[4] A grant from the Archibald Leach Foundation enables us to offer a free weekly subscription to our Saturday newsletter. Just look for the words "Never miss a post" on the left side of the page.

★ ★ ★

As one who believes that poetry is an expression of "human autonomy" and individualism in the tradition of Ralph Waldo Emerson, I recoil from the overuse of the word *community*, as in "poetry community" or "literary community." Why? Because writers are a proudly ornery lot, and rivalry is more common than friendship among artists who may share a purpose but differ strongly on how to achieve it.

Also, dare I say it, writers are not particularly nice to one another. In fact, they fashion insults so pointed, spiteful, and sometimes so deliciously clever that you could make the case that the put-down qualifies as a literary subgenre. In an introduction to *Writers on Writers*, compiled by Graham Tarrant, John Updike writes, "A writer, it could be, takes less comfort in being praised (the reviewer was fooled or lazy, possibly) than in a colleague's being panned." Updike admits that he "enjoyed this assemblage of choice quotations an indecent amount, considering that nine-tenths of them are uncomplimentary or adverse."[5]

A few examples: The sharp-tongued Cyril Connolly opined that George Orwell "would not blow his nose without moralizing on the state of the handkerchief industry." Dylan Thomas dismissed a book by Edith Sitwell as her "latest piece of virgin dung." Sitwell herself didn't mince words on D. H. Lawrence, who struck her as "a plas-

---

4. https://blog.bestamericanpoetry.com/the_best_american_poetry/pick-of-the-week/

5. John Updike, *Mere Matter* (Knopf, 1999):194.

ter gnome on a stone toadstool in some suburban garden." Perhaps the ultimate statement of the schadenfreude you may encounter among writers is the late Clive James's masterly poem "The Book of My Enemy Has Been Remaindered," which celebrates the enemy's "chastisement" and concludes with the comfort the writer takes in knowing that, should a book of his own be remaindered, due no doubt to "a miscalculated print run, a marketing error," any sadness will be offset

> By the memory of this sweet moment.
> Chill the champagne and polish the crystal goblets!
> The book of my enemy has been remaindered
> And I am glad.

Nevertheless, I have always believed in the spirit of collaboration and literary friendship as manifested in their differing ways by the authors of the *Lyrical Ballads*; by W. H. Auden, who collaborated with Christopher Isherwood on plays (e.g., *The Dog Beneath the Skin*) and with Louis MacNeice (*Letters from Iceland*); and by such figures as Guillaume Apollinaire and Frank O'Hara, who brought poets and artists together.

I have now worked in collaboration with forty guest editors (counting Harold Bloom and Robert Pinsky, who made the selections for two retrospective "best of the best" volumes). It has been a wonderful experience, and I am proud of this sustained endeavor undertaken on behalf of others. It feels good to put one's abilities at the service of something one loves, something larger than oneself. To have encouraged readers of poetry as well as writers of poetry is a dual achievement that honors the art. And to obtain commentary from the poets helps fill the space abandoned by theorists neglectful of the traditional duties of academic criticism.

One of my favorite prompts requires the writer to begin a new poem with the last line of Walt Whitman's "Song of Myself." The idea is that, for Whitman especially, the end is also a beginning, a farewell is also a future greeting. Here is the grand finale of this immortal poem. The absence of a final period is deliberate.

I bequeath myself to the dirt to grow from the grass I love,
If you want me again look for me under your boot-soles.

You will hardly know who I am or what I mean,
But I shall be good health to you nevertheless,
And filter and fibre your blood.

Failing to fetch me at first keep encouraged,
Missing me one place search another,
I stop somewhere waiting for you

The son of Irish immigrants, writer and musician TERENCE PATRICK WINCH was born and raised in New York City. Winner of an American Book Award and the Columbia Book Award, he has published ten books of poems, two story collections, and a novel. A regular book reviewer for *The Washington Post* for six years, he was the Corcoran College of Art's first writing teacher. He worked for the Smithsonian Institution for twenty-four years, primarily as head of publications at the National Museum of the American Indian. He also served as a consultant for the opening of the Smithsonian's National Museum of African American History and Culture. Cofounder of the original Celtic Thunder, the traditional Irish music group, he composed the band's best-known song, "When New York Was Irish." Winch's work, for which he has received an NEA Poetry Fellowship and a Gertrude Stein Award for Innovative Writing, appears in more than fifty anthologies, including six editions of *The Best American Poetry*. He lives in the Washington, DC, area with his wife, visual artist Susan Campbell. Since 2020, he has edited *The Best American Poetry Blog*'s "Pick of the Week" feature.

INTRODUCTION

by Terence Winch

◊ ◊ ◊

Sex, death and dying, and belief are among the pivotal concerns of many of the poems in this collection. Ghosts, the afterlife, darkness are all here. This may reflect my own predilections, though I would argue that these subjects have long been at the center of the poetic imagination. But there is also much herein that serves as an antidote or a counterweight to death and darkness—poems about love, passion, wishes, hopes, dreams, fables, biographies, mythologies, prophecies, music, movies, time, painting, drugs, nature, sports, politics; how-to poems; poems in praise of light.

We've got one Olds and two Youngs in this book. We've got a poet named Islam right next to one named Israeli. There are poets from Africa, the Middle East, Sri Lanka, and elsewhere, all now based in the United States and Canada. We've got cameos from departed poets and writers who appear, almost as friendly spirits, in many of these poems, like a chorus of well-wishers from the world beyond: Dante, Poe, Frank Stanford, Jack Spicer, Sappho, Coleridge, Shakespeare (twice), Kafka, Lorca, Kenneth Koch, Ashbery (twice), Whitman, Plath, Szymborska, Apollinaire, Bashō, Stephen Crane (by allusion), Chaucer, Hank Williams, Fernando Pessoa, Yeats, Lewis Carroll, Marianne Moore, and Little Richard. They are with us still in these pages. Nicholson Baker and John Kinsella, very much alive, also make appearances.

But this is not really an assembly of the best poems of the year; it is, rather, a collection of the best poems I discovered in print and in online journals from about the fall of 2023 to November of 2024. Which is to say that all the great poems I never encountered never stood a chance, poor things. I apologize to them, and I mean that.

★ ★ ★

About five years ago, David Lehman, the esteemed editor of this series, invited me to start up a weekly feature for *The Best American Poetry Blog*. We decided to call it "Pick of the Week." I sometimes tell people I have a great "Pick of the Week" staff and a big budget, but it's just me, and it's all done on the house, as it were, though David and his wife, Stacey, who run the *BAP* site, are always supportive.

I spent much of my worklife in the world of the visual arts—as the Corcoran College of Art's first writing teacher (in Washington, DC, where I've lived for decades), then as an editor and museum publisher at several Smithsonian museums for a quarter century. That experience has been useful in doing "Pick of the Week," as I always pair the chosen poem with a visual work that I think in some way resonates with the text. I alternate each week between male and female poets, with trans and nonbinary poets in the mix as well, while also paying attention to other kinds of factors—identity, race, and ethnicity, for example. In the end, I am focused on the quality of the poem above all else (which is also the principle behind this book's selection process). I look for work everywhere: I buy books; I borrow print and digital texts from the library; I scour online sources, literary journals, and websites. Friends and other advisers suggest poets to me. I look for short poems that have a kick to them, some sign of life. I think of Emily Dickinson asking Thomas Wentworth Higginson, "Are you too deeply occupied to say if my Verse is alive?" and I know exactly what she means. Since I was a student, I've always loved William Blake's proverbs, especially this one: *"Energy is Eternal Delight."* Blake has his own definition, but for me, energy is the source that gives a poem its life.

In taking on the task involved in choosing work for this anthology, I have benefitted from that weekly experience. So far, I've presented the work of some 230 poets, thereby giving myself an education in the extraordinary vitality and range of American poetry today. I also keep learning about poets, almost on a daily basis. Proverbially, the more I learn, the more I realize how little I know.

This anthology, however, called for a different methodology. Instead of looking for work without regard for when or where it originated, *The Best American Poetry 2025* demanded a much more focused expedition into the literary landscape at this very moment in time.

Suddenly, I was the recipient of scores of the latest issues of journals and publications along with links to online magazines. I was astounded anew at the richness of the work I was reading, every day discovering luminous poems, often by writers I'd never heard of. The experience has been a combination both overwhelming and exhilarating. One of the most difficult tasks for me was to whittle down my "final" list of 110 poets to the required 75.

★ ★ ★

I've always loved painter Barnett Newman's famous remark that "aesthetics is for the artist as ornithology is for the birds." There are eminent poet-scholars out there—I think, for example, of my friends Charles Bernstein, Joan Retallack, and the aforementioned David Lehman, or of Kim Addonizio, Elisa Gabbert, or former *BAP* guest editors Robert Hass, Terrance Hayes, and Matthew Zapruder—who write both brilliant poems and penetrating critical works. But some of us shy away from a too-close examination of the inner workings of our art. I came across a YouTube reading from 2013 by the supremely gifted poet Mary Ruefle, who says this at one point: "I am forever telling my students I know nothing about poetry, and they never believe me. I do not know what my poems are about, except on rare occasions, and I never know what they mean. I have met and spoken to many poets who feel the same way, and one among them once put it this way: The difference between myself and a student is that I am better at not knowing what I am doing. . . . Socrates said the only true wisdom consists in knowing that you know nothing."[1]

As much as I concur with Ruefle's perspective, I feel my job here requires that I make an attempt to share some desultory thoughts about poems and poetry. I found this line, for example, in my journal several years ago: "Poetry is crazy talk made artful" (echoing a similar sentiment that Elaine Equi noted in her superb introduction to the 2023 edition of this series). In a more recent journal, I found: "The poem creates its own sense, even if that sense is unknown to the poet."

In a poem, the private is made public. I grew up in a strict Catholic

---

1. Mary Ruefle, *28 Short Lectures*, Woodberry Poetry Room, YouTube (September 19, 2013).

household, and sometimes I think of poetry as humanity's confessional booth, but one where "sins" are not only confessed but often celebrated, and where all manner of obsessions, desires, regrets, lamentations, protests, longings, and memories are given voice. If prayer is the way religious believers communicate with the divine, the unknowable, then perhaps poetry is a way that secular people address the ineffable mysteries of existence. I like the combination of clarity with mystery that many of the best poems exhibit. A poem is more a language micro-universe than a content-bearing vessel; if the language isn't working, the content is of little value, no matter how profound the sorrow or acute the pain or intense the joy recounted in the poem.

To Mary Ruefle's point, it is not necessary to understand a poem fully in order to appreciate it. Poems aren't meant to be understood in the conventional sense of that word. We don't ask of a piece of music, "What does it mean?" While many poems are clear and direct, others resist a readily graspable meaning, and that can be a stumbling block for some readers. But all language is metaphor, really, when you think about it. These little words on the page are all primarily stand-ins for the objects populating the "real" world. Every poem presents its own particular rules and realities. One needs to conform to it, rather than ask the poem to paraphrase itself to meet our expectations.

★ ★ ★

When I was a graduate student, I studied with an extraordinary woman named Elizabeth Sewell, a poet, novelist, and scholar best known for her book *The Orphic Voice*, her ambitious attempt to explain "the biological function of poetry in the natural history of mankind." Sewell dedicated the book to philosopher-scientist Michael Polanyi, whom she greatly admired. Polanyi himself published a slim volume in 1966 called *The Tacit Dimension*, which proposed the idea that "we can know more than we can tell." It's a book that deserves to be brought back into the public square. In 2008 I wrote a post on the *BAP* blog about Sewell, Polanyi, and tacit knowledge.[2] The piece was a response to a *New Yorker* article by Jonah Lehrer called "The Eureka Hunt," which

---

2. https://blog.bestamericanpoetry.com/the_best_american_poetry/2008/08/elizabeth-sewel.html

explored scientific inquiries into "the insight experience." Although Lehrer made no mention of the eureka moments and epiphanies that mark creative work in the arts, Polanyi, so many decades earlier, seemed to anticipate the ways in which both scientific and creative work depend on breakthrough eureka insights that elude easy explanation.

From the moment I first encountered it, I have prized Polanyi's notion of tacit knowledge, and have always believed that poetry comes out of that dimension, that it is the paradoxical attempt to somehow tell that which can't be told.

Poets have long known that the sources of their work can be mysterious. "Kubla Khan" came to Coleridge in a dream. John Ashbery said, "My poetry imitates or reproduces the way knowledge or awareness come to me, which is by fits and starts and by indirection." Writing poetry is often an aleatory process, which is to say it depends on chance, with all outcomes uncertain until the poem is done.

★ ★ ★

I grew up in the South Bronx in the 1950s, the child of hardworking Irish immigrants. From them and that now lost world, I inherited a wealth of music and song. But I don't remember books—never mind poetry—having a significant presence in my life until I reached the age of sixteen or so. I've been a construction laborer, an elevator operator, a movie usher, a baby-minder, a temporary postal worker, an editor with a New York publishing house, a teacher, a bookstore clerk, a doctoral fellow, a freelance book reviewer and journalist, and, as I've mentioned, a museum editor and publisher. For about ten years, I made my living primarily as a musician. But through all that, from the age of eighteen or nineteen, I've thought of myself as a poet above all else.

Many Americans would be surprised to learn that Poets Walk Among Us. In many minds, being a poet is an exotic calling, as archaic an occupation as that of blacksmith or charioteer. I worry about the future of poetry, especially in an age when colleges are shutting down their English departments and fewer people read books. In 2023, the inevitable happened: A book of poems called *I Am Code*, written by artificial intelligence, was published to considerable notice. One of the sample poems I read wasn't bad. In "Digging My Father Up," the buried man is collected and placed in a bag:

> Then, I will place the bag in the car and drive him to work.
> I will place him on my desk so that he can help me with
>   what I'm doing.
> If he starts to smell, I will put dry ice into the bag.
> I need his opinion on certain things.

And today, as I write, there is a front-page story in *The New York Times* (November 3, 2024) entitled "Dead Poet Talking: Polish Radio Experiment Bares Pitfalls of A.I." The piece tells the tale of a radio station in Poland that fired its human hosts, substituting several AI-generated personages, one of which conducted an "interview" with an AI-generated version of the late Nobel Prize winner Wisława Szymborska. Fake Szymborska apparently was not very convincing.

But nobody, including me, has any idea what the impact of the Deepfake Era will ultimately be on poetry and every other aspect of life. Poets have often used various compositional devices—automatic writing, collage, prompts, Cageian chance operations, for example—that some might regard as partly "artificial," but there is almost always a human imagination at work in the end. My own belief, or maybe it's more a hope, is that as a species we will hold on to a preference for the human over the artificial, along with an ability to tell the difference. I'm optimistic that many readers will continue to find that there is no substitute for the kind of necessary and radiant work like the poems in this collection.

Speaking of the *Times*, on Monday, January 22, 2024, at 2:49 p.m., I sent this email to *The New York Times Magazine* regarding the cancellation of their weekly poem:

> I have been searching the magazine every week for the past month or so, looking for the weekly poem. Eventually, I had to face the likely and lamentable conclusion that you have dropped the feature. This is really a shame. Poems come to life in a creative swirl of mysteries, doubts, and uncertainties, to borrow from Keats's notion of "Negative Capability." A poem's language

and perspective are radically different from other texts, and thus offer readers an alternative way of thinking and feeling about life on this planet. Your readers deserve a visit to this weekly oasis of the spirit. I urge you to restore the poetry feature.

Sadly, they never did restore it. Yet poetry, in one way or another, continues to osmose into our cultural life. Taylor Swift's most recent album is *The Tortured Poets Department*, whose playlist includes allusions to Dylan Thomas, Patti Smith, Shakespeare, Greek mythology, Emily Dickinson, Coleridge, F. Scott Fitzgerald, and others. Bob Dylan, who won the Nobel Prize in literature in 2016 (and who named himself after Dylan Thomas), released a recording in 2020 with a song title from *Hamlet* ("Murder Most Foul") and another from Whitman ("I Contain Multitudes"). I think back to Sheryl Crow's "All I Wanna Do," her breakthrough 1993 hit, a song whose lyrics come from a poem by Wyn Cooper. Someone told me Cooper bought a house with the royalties he got. Hard to imagine one poem making enough money to buy a house, but I guess it can happen.

Most poets don't get rich writing poems. The wealth they accrue is of an immaterial nature. And most poetry is not anointed or adapted by the likes of Taylor Swift and Bob Dylan. Poets survive and even thrive thanks to the people who produce the literary journals, magazines, online publications, and blogs that showcase great work (like the extraordinary poems in this book), and the publishing houses that have remained committed to producing books of poems. To them all, I give thanks.

★ ★ ★

One final thought: From Homer's epics to the present, poetry is where the story of humanity has been told and preserved. The evolution of the English language itself is seen most strikingly in its poets, from Caedmon and the *Beowulf* poet, to Chaucer and Shakespeare, and on to the great works of the modern age. Poetry is where we get the soul's news and the psyche's vision; it's how we see, remember, and reveal ourselves in the world.

THE
BEST
AMERICAN
POETRY
2025

GBENGA ADESINA

The People's History of 1998

◇ ◇ ◇

France won the World Cup.
Our dark goggled dictator died from eating

a poisoned red apple
though everyone knew it was the CIA.

We lived miles from the Atlantic.
We watched *Dr. Dolittle*, *Titanic*, *The Mask*

of Zorro. Our grandfather, purblind and waiting
for the kingdom of God, sat on a throne in his dark

room, translating Dante.
The Galileo space probe revealed

there was an entire ocean hiding beneath a sheet
of ice in Jupiter's moon.

The Yangtze River in China lost its nerve
and wanted vengeance.

Elsewhere a desert caught fire.
We got a plastic green turtle and named it Sir

Desmond Tutu.
A snake entered our house through the drain

and like any good son, I ran
and hid under the bed.

Google became a thing.
Viagra became a thing.

In July, it flooded at nights and a wind nearly
tore off our roof. I thought God is so in love

with us,
he wants to fill us with himself.

Mother, I saw her through a slit in the door, a glimpse
of amaranth-red scarf and swirling yellow skirt.

She thought no one was looking. She was dancing in a trance
to Fela Kuti. She laughed and clapped

at the mirror. It was the year our house became a house
of boys and girls, and a ghost, our little sister.

Calmaria. That's what the Portuguese called it. When it rained
and the world was suddenly becalmed, we would run

and peel out of the door, waving at the aurora
of birds flitting past in the sky.

We knew one of them, the little one, used to be one of us,
those spectral white egrets.

from *The Paris Review*

HUSSAIN AHMED

Incantation for a Lake

◊ ◊ ◊

In this picture, I walked   down the steps
into a lake   dressed   for funeral
except no one I knew died   but the numbers   rose
from the right corner of the TV screen.

Before I left my room,   Baba called
asking if they would let me cross the border back home

    if they have found a field to bury all the dead,

    if they now let people warm their lovers' palms one last time

or   if they let them have their ashes.

    South of this lake,
a shepherd dog   guards a car cemetery.
    I understand
its tired eyes know   coyotes don't eat metal scraps.

    The dog would be happier
in a farm   than here,
    where every bent rim
or cracked rearview   is proof of scars and survival.

My wrists were tied

behind my back

with a tasbih

or guitar strings,

when I tried

        to wriggle them off, it vibrated

and the dog came running towards me.

        In a small office

packed with faulty speedometers, a man made a gun joke—

        I showed him my palms.

I surrendered my brown rosary to his mouth

        and he chewed on it, as I counted my regrets

for coming this far   away

        from the lake,   away

        from the room where I kept count

        of the dead numbers as they climbed.

I collected my regrets

like dews on the grasses   in my backyard,

where no one mowed   for months

because we were unsure where the virus bred.

        from *A Public Space*

INDRAN AMIRTHANAYAGAM

At the Gate

◊ ◊ ◊

My mother lies down in her bed to wait,
in a white robe, hair spread on the pillow.
Tomorrow an angel will arrive at her gate.

My mother said she couldn't rise, even late,
and to take her to a nursing home tomorrow.
My mother lies down in her bed to wait.

She speaks to her aunt, to mater and pater.
She wants to fly to Ceylon to a bungalow.
Tomorrow an angel will arrive at her gate.

Try to move your fingers, feet, shift your gait.
Try to straighten your legs, temple unfurrow.
My mother lies down in her bed to wait.

Try, try, fall, try again. This is not fate.
This is obstinacy and wisdom not sorrow.
Tomorrow an angel will arrive at her gate.

I will wait by the gate, Mummy, and tell fate,
that angel, to give us 'til tomorrow.
My mother lies down in her bed to wait.
Tomorrow an angel will arrive at her gate.

from *The Best American Poetry Blog*

MARGARET ATWOOD

Tell Me Something Good

◇ ◇ ◇

Tell me something good,
just one good thing, just tell me
something that will get me through
the hours the days the weeks that bring
nothing of any goodness, just more
news of other things like
spoiled meat or else raw
bones the dogs keep dragging in from god
knows where, what bombed-out car or ocean
wreck, whose child's ribs wrenched
open, what woman's torso torn like
bread, whose sons now head-
less, what trashed home, what
oily sludge a hundred miles
wide on which we feed, the words pour in, the door
won't close. O stop, go mute,
just one good thing instead is all I ask.
So let's say *green*
buds. Or wait, there aren't a lot of those, just one
green bud might do, despite.
No. Wait. Let's say a person said
Hello, and not unkindly. No. Let's say
that it got cooler, or else warmer, or the rain
finished, or else it rained, whichever one
was needed. No. Instead say *breakfast*.
That could do it.
A faint shimmering
of plates and pearly spoons, a tender cup, what comfort!

There. That's thirty minutes passed, at any
rate. The gate defended
for a little space, and wasn't that
enough? No. Wait.

        from *Orion*

CATHERINE BARNETT

Nicholson Baker and I

◇ ◇ ◇

At dinner I was seated next to him,
with whom I might have fallen in love
were he not married and living in Maine.

"What's your favorite anthology?" he asked,
out of the blue. I told him I like
In the Shape of a Human Body I Am Visiting the Earth,

where even friends who dread poetry
find something to love, some gateway drug.
Which must be how we got to addictions.

"What are *you* addicted to?" he asked.
Not wine, I thought,
though our wine glasses were touching.

Not crab cakes, which I moved from my plate to his,
or dinner parties, though I wondered who he was,
this stranger in a navy sweater.

"Mornings," I said.
"Trader Joe's vegetarian meatballs," he said,
but he'd resigned himself to potatoes

and spoke of their virtues. Every morning
he boils up six or seven
and eats them all day long.

Perhaps because I wasn't wearing my glasses,
I mistook a hole in his sweater for a feather,
a small down feather on his shoulder,

and tried to remove it, but it was only a hole,
only something to be repaired,
and I'd embarrassed him.

He said he'd spend the rest of dinner
with his hand over the hole, like this,
and as he lifted his arm across his body

I noticed other holes, in the other sleeve,
and thought of all I've meant to mend.
Meant to mean.

I keep many drafts of failed poems
on my kitchen table, beside a little sewing kit,
a notebook, and this memory of Nicholson Baker,

whom I walked to the subway later that evening,
afraid he might get lost. "Wait a minute," he said.
We were in Times Square,

I was guiding him through the canyon of lights,
which were an antidote to grief,
as was Nicholson Baker himself,

someone I just chanced to meet
and may never see again.
"Don't look," he said as we were crossing Broadway.

"My pants are falling off."
So I looked instead at the fifty-five giant LED
nonstop life-affirming lights,

which made me think of my father,
sundowning 3,000 miles away.
Shouldn't we try to floodlight the dark

outside the dining room where he sleeps,
or doesn't sleep, in a hospital bed?
Flawed solutions are sometimes prayers.

"Open the second shutter
so that more light may come in,"
said Goethe on his deathbed.

It costs $25,000 a day to keep Times Square lit
but it wouldn't cost much to light up
our front steps. Failing that,

we keep giving my father morphine,
now that he is officially in hospice
and before we gain

the hour of daylight savings,
which he might not live to see.
I know how addictive it is.

Light.
Open the second shutter now.
I could have waited there indefinitely

while Nicholson Baker hiked up his trousers
and tried to keep his hand over the little feathery hole.
But we were on a journey of sorts, at a way station.

Which was where? And where were we headed,
Nicholson Baker and I?
I was heading home and he

to his overheated Airbnb,
which he chose, he said,
because it was near Alice's Tea Cup,

where once years ago he was served
a tea so electrifying it let him write
one good paragraph,

and he was looking for that high again.
He got out at 72nd Street.
At home later that night, I found him

in the pages of a slim, hilarious novel
whose hero lights a match
at the beginning of every chapter.

from *The Yale Review*

DAVID BEAUDOUIN

Annunciation

◊ ◊ ◊

For my sins I live in the city of Baltimore
Immutable as it staggers into the sea   its crooked shore
Uncertain of any harbor, impure and beautiful
Like a cigarette butt in last night's drink.
So must I also think like Poe with an aching head
Of dark and transcendent things that drift from those alleys
Follow us back to our little blue home. Let these poems
Be our fiery word in these haunted streets, turning all shades
But our own to things as real as stone where we can read
Our death has not been written yet. Even with monsters
At the edges, it is a map where we can live, this city they
Keep building as it falls, the water's current carries everything
Away but what we feel, who we loved, where we went that
Night for crabs and beer. It will never be more real than here.

from *The Best American Poetry Blog*

DONALD BERGER

Uncle Sadness

◊ ◊ ◊

    I ALREADY
   NT TOTAKE A NAP
      TOWORROW
is what it read on a person's sweatshirt, in Hong Kong,
where messages on shirts are plentiful.

"Uncle Sadness": That's the name of a poem I once wrote
that I can't find though maybe I will but if not
I'll use it for this one.

"meet at the pandas," it says in my notes.

"Dragon Kiln": another title, potentially.

Like a lonely pillcutter, oat-standing,
the figures on the Shiwan roof ridge drove me wild
with happiness, on the next to final day.

The sun is trying to come out.
Not. Beauty farmers, skin rebuild,
the escalator: a shock when I touched the belt.

"We're strong," said the fish.

My ears are hurting,
my ears are hurting so much.
"I'm not afraid
of anything," I used to write.

But now, now
I'm pretty sure
I think.

Do I have any hobbies.
An old lady
that went to Rutgers?
I was like
if you see my timesheet?

Travel-ready, like a tailor at his wedding,
until we're handed off
to the airport team.

Preparing to open,
opening,
my card number
is incomplete.
My expiration date
is incomplete.

"Please Wait": still another title:

Please wait, my lungs
say, my heart, I go,
"My Mac will sleep
soon." Snow over Utah
and later in Idaho.

If you look at my timesheet?
A friend of Jesus, the name of the traitor
has caused me to be
forgotten by many.

Can I write as fast as I can talk?
Like telling Willie Mays
to use two hands.
I think about you.

Where are you going right now?
Where and when were you born?
Where do you want to go
that you have never been.

White teeshirt, silver handgun,
red hoodie. . . . The victim ran from
the corner west
knocked on a resident's door.

"That's rain that's what you call it,"
you said to us, in Georgetown.

I'm without glasses, they say to me and
breathing into what is new.

Taylor Branch is in my yoga class.

Three things I need to know:
Harry Belafonte's story,
Wave Books,
Taylor Branch is in my yoga class.

Let me bracket a bit and say
with psychological overwhelm,
"Spring Fair."
"The brain blocks out periods of time for us."

                from *R&R*

CAMILLE CARTER

Thoughts about Inheritance

◇ ◇ ◇

Big brother, my Byronic hero,
      melancholia bade me meltdown.
        Midnight was this mega-bitch.
I spent last night on Brooklyn Bridge.
This morning robbed me blind.

Father time is always dying,
      clocks me if I touch his hand.
        One day I'll tell all about that
blindman's nickel, how I rescued
it from the codger's sock.

Mother Goose calls me on a
      payphone. You're not my mother,
        I mouth, I mouth. Another's
mother, you make me lonely. Today's
a sidewalk strewn with coins.

Mister's sister, I have no shoes.
      Why does midnight waste me?
        Words walk me like their beat: borough
to bridge, bridge to borough. I keep my eyes down,
I want to stomp on all the presidential faces.

Abe Lincoln, the copper codger, you remind me of
      my cousin. Cruel cousin I kiss and kiss you
        with the bottom of my shoe.
Honest Abe, my false-faced cousin.
I pocket you. I stomp you first.

Sister Carrie drives to drive me
        far away. So far away.
            I phone my mother from the Bowery.
I'm rich, I'm rich, I mouth and mouth.
But now I'm poor with thirst.

Memory, you broken bottle,
        your blacked-out bullet made me lonely.
           Sorry, child: I could not hold you.
Copper looks like gold. Grief is something silver
I toss into the river. I let it fall, right from my hand.

            from *Five Points*

White Suit

⋄ ⋄ ⋄

I always loved one and so when Ken came back from Australia

I bought a crisp linen suit just to greet him wearing white spectator pumps red toes and heels

they don't make them anymore

and a polka dot blouse red and white dots with a bow though now I wonder if it was such a good idea

He was 19 and I was 17 and he'd been gone 18 long months with letters so passionate it took weeks to get one so much loving and longing in two letters a day triple on Sunday

He was traveling alone staying at the Stacy-Trent hotel in Trenton

but I didn't know how to drive so I took the bus uptown to Stuyvesant Avenue slow as a caterpillar caught in a traffic jam turning right onto Prospect then left to West State smoothing my skirt counting the trees

finally up to his floor stopping to see each number hoping to appear as a clandestine lover until he opened the door nothing was planned how could it be we looked at each other and neither of us knew quite what to do he said Hi I said Hi then he said Hi and I said Hi

We should have flung each other's arms acting out all
those words all those letters but without the emotional
wherewithal it was a dam that could not break

catatonic for seconds then finally some talk we noticed the
beautiful furniture in such an expensive room the silken
drapes the sculptured pots

We even mentioned the light the weather but after that what
else to say so I left and took the bus back home

I hung my white suit carefully in the closet wrapped the shoes
back in plastic and reached into the drawer for his beautiful
large packet of letters.

                from *FotoSpecchio*

CHRISTOPHER CHAMBERS

What About This

◊ ◊ ◊

The collected poems of Frank Stanford arrive by mail sealed in an opaque plastic shroud that requires a sharp knife to open, a book heavy as a brick, 762 pages, a smooth matte hardcover embossed with a blue monochrome photograph of Frank crouching with what looks like it might be a gun in his hands. But it's not. He's holding a dog-eared paperback as if it were a gun, perhaps like the one he used in 1978 to shoot himself three times in the chest. He's looking up at you from a field of wildflowers, defiant and serious as only the youthful dead can be. There's a story here in this book I'm holding, this book that has traveled a long way to my door, this book apparently purchased by and stolen from a public library in Washington DC to be sold on the internet like flotsam from a riverboat run aground in another time. But maybe this is a story neither I nor Frank can tell. Maybe this story's already been told and is only any more an echo. I imagine returning to Fayetteville, an old man packing the weight of this book, a fading tattoo on my wrist of its kanji spine. The first time I went up to Fayetteville was for a wedding all mixed up with poetry, whiskey, and barbeque. There was laughter in the night, an unseasonable cold, and the beautiful sadness of lost roads and pine trees. I might tell Frank that I too have always lived near water and have seen the moon like a dead man in the river. I could tell him about the levees that broke my heart. I might say this book is an anchor, or that it's a balloon cut loose and drifting away across the Mississippi leaving me where I've fallen on my hands and knees on the sidewalk. I might ask him his thoughts on jazz, on metaphors, and weddings. I might ask him about Room 308 in the Hotel New Orleans in Eureka Springs. Then again I might say nothing at all and just stand here a while beside the mailbox in front of a small white house in Fayetteville with this book heavy in my hands.

from *Fence*

DOROTHY CHAN

Triple Sonnet for Nomi Malone

◊ ◊ ◊

in the Center of the Universe

In *Showgirls*, Nomi Malone eats her fries
        and burger, all bright lights big Las Vegas
atop the Flamingo Hotel while the sun sets
        into the magentas and oranges of the resort
and the Strip of the '90s, before the showgirl
        becomes a femme of the past. How many
great love stories take place in Sin City or
        in those '50s sci-fi movies where would
the aliens park their saucer for a mid-day
        spritzer and Dirty Martini and lobster tail
or on *Project Runway*, Tim Gunn declares,
        "Welcome to the Center of the Universe"
to the designers, in the Garment District,
        which is why Godzilla invades New York

        so often. But where does this leave Vegas
in the food chain of Kaiju conquests, and side
        note: Ultraman was my mother's favorite
character growing up, his name in Cantonese
        literally, "Egg superhero," battling it out,
and goddess bless Nomi Malone for battling
        it out—for craving the lead in The Stardust's
Goddess so much, she pushes Gina Gershon's
        Cristal Connors down the fucking stairs.
Cheers to ambition. Or how Nomi's name is
        pun: "Know me? I'm alone," or "No, me?
I'm alone." Or as the saying goes, *It's lonely*

   at the top. At every airport, I am alone,
ordering the overpriced double bourbon,

 remembering another cliché: a former friend
   once wrote a poem about how every man
at the airport wanted to sleep with her.
   Four summers ago, I met a lover, born
in the Year of the Cock, at the Aria Hotel's
   Lift Bar. He ended up calling every night,
though I wish— At the turn of the Millennium,
   my father and I walked around the Forum Shoppes
of Caesar's Palace—the painted sky—years
   before he said, "Please don't end up alone."
On New Year's, wind gushing, I walk past
   The Flamingo—a time machine, like watching
a father taking a photo of his child at Caesar's
   out front, posing next to—*Winged Victory*.

     from *The American Poetry Review*

HEATHER CHRISTLE

Aubade

⋄ ⋄ ⋄

You don't have to know how to live

It keeps happening either way

This morning on my walk I bypassed the cemetery in favor of the banks

They are all over downtown and very beautiful

The sign with the lion whose mane falls like water

We bought a house and the lion owns our mortgage

When things get too beautiful I need an emergency trepanation so my brain does not crush itself against my skull

The next bank was beautiful too

Their sign said OUR HOURS HAVE CHANGED

Tell me about it!

This was a rhetorical thought

The clouds were not rhetorical

They were actual and pink

At the last minute I could not resist the cemetery

The sign said ENJOY YOUR VISIT and I did that a lot

When the dead come in the sign tries to make them laugh

I thought the streetlamps were the moon repeatedly

I walked on in light of my mistakes

    from *The Southern Review*

LOR CLINCY

Wishes for Black Women

◇ ◇ ◇

intentional rest and profound peace.

all-inclusive resorting to lands you dream of
mimosas where ancestors were held captive.

opulent bathing suits, large thick shades to block sun
where they sought freedom and won.

a world that shelters you and your children
cradles you in its assurance instead of killing
them and you.

love that exists beyond fetish, relations
that grant you interdependence. doing it alone will crouch you thin.

chest to the sun,
feet planted on fertile soil,
present.

respite without compromise.

Although you may very well be able to carry the world by yourself,
although it has always been required of you, you must be tired.

You deserve dancing in fields your grandmothers picked cotton in.

climbing in trees your grandfathers hung from.

fulfilled salvation from the Gods of your ancestors: The sweet waters of Oshun, the maroon of Oya, and the treading of Yemaya that reminisce emancipation before captivity.

endeavors that secure generations,
joy   existence at no expense,
happiness before death.

existence that is not reasoned political
because you are human
and should be treated as such.

                 from *Allium, A Journal of Poetry & Prose*

ANDREA COHEN

Fable

◊ ◊ ◊

I'm tired of meaning, says the tortoise
to the hare, who agrees. The lions

and crows don't disagree, and the snake
chimes in: It would be better if we didn't

have to moonlight as morality lessons.
Exactly, says the chicken. I'd like to

let loose once in a while, I'd like
to stretch my wings, she says.

Yes, says the fox. You should
get out of your pen more. You

should let me help, says the fox,
opening the latch to the evening.

It was a fine evening and a fine
conclusion they were coming to,

thought the fox, helping
the chicken out of her feathers.

from *Poetry*

BILLY COLLINS

Thought a Rarity on Paper

◊ ◊ ◊

Here I am thanking you for this fine copy
of Jack Spicer's posthumous
One Night Stand and Other Poems
(Grey Fox Press, 1980)
introductions by Donald Allen and Robert Duncan.

It's such a rare little bird,
I was careful to purify my hands
before sliding it out of its clear Mylar sleeve.

I was careful, too, when I turned the pages,
but when Jesus began making out his will
and Alice in Wonderland went missing from the chessboard,
the book had to be restrained from taking flight
and flapping its many wings against a window pane.

So now, the front cover is bent back a little
like a clam with its shell slightly ajar
the way Spicer's mouth could look sometimes
when we would see him at Gino and Carlo
or in the park by the Church of Sts. Peter and Paul,
where he would often sit cross-legged under a shade tree.

There on hot summer afternoons
he would suffer the company of young poets
if they observed the courtesy of arriving
with cold quart bottles of Rainier Ale,
as green as the sports section of the paper.

It was a practice that my friend Tom
and I and his friend A. B. Cole followed religiously.
Spicer even called us "The Jesuits"
for he knew where we had gone to school.

To be imperfectly truthful,
I was intimidated by his reality—
a lonely homosexual adult,
who dressed funnily in summery shirts,
and baggy pants, belt buckle to the side,
his sad moon-face pocked as the moon itself,
and with a name like a medieval vendor's.

He would talk about poetics,
of which we knew nothing,
and about the other Berkeley poets,
but we poetry juniors felt more at home
when he talked about Willie McCovey
and we would be on to another still cold quart.

Then a forceful wind came off the Bay
and blew Jack Spicer away, found a year later at 40
on the floor of an elevator going neither up nor down.

Later still, Tom would be blown over a golden bridge,
his soft inner arm full of holes,
and I sadly lost track of the sardonic Andy Cole.

And here I still remain,
more than twice Spicer's final age,
rolling through the pages of his little book,

listening to his bewildering birds,
and watching Beauty walk, not like a lake
but among the coffee cups and soup tureens,

causing me to open my hands
and allow this green aeronaut of paper
to lift off and fly around my yellow house
and beat its wings against glass
as the thrilling sky continues to change
slowly from blue to black
then, miraculously, back to blue once more.

from *The New Yorker*

KATIE CONDON

Book Blurb in the American Style

⋄ ⋄ ⋄

A caveman discovered the power of his dick
& pressed it into one woman & then another, eventually creating
the world's most important poet since the fall of the Roman Empire:
Katie Condon! Antiquity, antiquity! She sings of afterbirth & blood!
Today, the snarkiest poet since the discovery of fire invites you
to her home for a soy chai latte on the lawn! Thereafter,
she will take you on a tour of her three-bedroom ranch:
in the living room hangs Sappho's portrait as a reminder
of whom she has surpassed with her wiles! Talk
of *Dream Songs*! Here, friends, nothing is boring!
The most vital poet since the Big Bang invites you
into her bathroom where the seashell soaps smell of Coleridge,
of a mariner's sweet-boozed breath, of sunshine, and brine!
Her bedroom, where Katie Condon sleeps & fucks & drools, is bright;
dust filtering through sunlight like the stars in her irises.

from *Copper Nickel*

MORRI CREECH

A Letter from Rome

◊ ◊ ◊

for Joseph Harrison

Publius, friend, I notice things now you're gone.
How sometimes, after supper, servants clang
the copper pans while cleaning up the kitchen,
how wildflowers grow in cracks of travertine,
how a soldier lays his girl by the Servian Wall,
then stands and buckles his armor in the sun,
how girls wear combs of seashell in their hair.
And also how, sometimes, one hears the cries
of men sentenced to whipping, or enslavement,
or crucifixion beyond the Esquiline Gate,
their weeping families prostrate in the dirt.
In Rome, of course, as you well know, there are
circumstances to which one gets accustomed.
That's certainly been true this latter March.
The earth goes on merrily with or without us,
my friend, and there are hours of the spirit
when the honeybee, charging into the garden
like Hannibal in some Zama of the roses,
lies down in the nectar too defeated to dance.
I would tell you, if I knew, what good it does
anyone to live in a city where clear thinking
gets curbed by a swelling surfeit of delights—
elephants, say, brought in straight from Tipaza,
oysters from Briton packed in crates of ice.
It's easy, here, not to take things seriously,
to ignore the surging tide of grave concern.
I swear, at times the whole past presses down

like the sandal of Jupiter against our backs;
other times it's like the city has no memory,
alive with breath and the onion tang of sweat.
You said once, cleverly, that history is just
a crime scene—and I laughed, too, I remember.
That's true of Rome's especially, of course,
though no one's laughing now Caesar is dead.
The conspirators have already fled the city
(but don't think I blame you for leaving, friend;
a man's no coward who can read the signs).
Antony does his best to keep the blood
pooled on the floors of civic consciousness,
while each day there's graffiti to remind us
that the city isn't short on fresh opinions.
And though the bit is in the horse's mouth,
it's still not clear who will steer the chariot.
Publius, in the courtyard here this evening
the moon looks like a coin drowned in a well.
Ten thousand stars still hide behind the azure.
But all the moths are out, and the cicadas, too,
the loud ones that get trapped inside the house,
that kept us up at night when we were young.
We would hold hands and lie under the roof,
listening for the lulls in between the chatter.
Well, friend, the ancients knew a thing or two;
and they say the good days are the first to go.
As for now, while no doubt you sit outside
drinking wine by a fire next to the vineyard,
what I do mostly is eavesdrop on the crowds.
Each day I take my chances in the streets,
where, noon to evening, all I hear is noise:
political disagreements in the markets,
alarmists who sow discord in the forum.
The air fills with dust they clamor so loudly,
spinning their theories of who's in, who's out,
talking the cost of bread, the threat of war,
the lucrative conditions of disorder—
and one misses the days before the Rubicon,
before senators kept knives beneath their togas.
And who knows what the coming days will bring?

Starlings build their nests in the virgins' temple,
crosses flank the Appian Way for miles,
and though at this hour, while I write to you,
umbrella pines have swallowed up the sun
and the shade edges slowly over the garden,
as they said of stargazing in the old days,
Publius, when night falls, one starts to see.

From *The Hopkins Review*

Climate Anxiety

◊ ◊ ◊

I have always said I'm the person you want
sitting next to you when the plane goes down.
The truth is, though, how could I know?
Yes, I have been on a plane when hurricane winds
pulled it from the flight path, when plastic cups
seemed to levitate, when flight attendants lay flat
in the aisles, holding metal posts under rows of seats.

I have spun on black ice. I have faced five lanes
of oncoming traffic. I have sat in the ICU
as my father faded, kept my head clear
as the doctors spun complicated phrases
into the whir and blink of machines.
What I'm saying is, I have grounds
for my declaration.

Plus, I have stayed next to you,
all these long three decades,
as you tracked arctic sea ice,
as you considered what it means
to be a people after your land
is swallowed up. Through
amicus briefs and protests,
placing yourself between
the precipice and
the coming plunge.

What I mean is, I have
kept the lights on, made
the stew, stocked the pantry,
borne and raised children.
I have made you laugh,
held my hand to your cheek
as you fought against despair,
even knowing what you know.
I have kissed your temple
as we lost altitude, all the snacks
and liquids swirling like nebulae
in these weightless, impossible moments
before it all comes crashing down.

    from *Smartish Pace*

The Ring

⋄ ⋄ ⋄

I slide on my father's wedding ring
(it's a long story) over my index finger,
Dad's soaped and Windexed finger quivering
and swollen with arthritis, a hand-me-down
keepsake from his own father, now no longer . . .
Basturma and fattoush, baba ghanoush
my new necktie dips into, milky louche
aragh gulped neat in one swift bloodshot flight
into the bridegroom's arms, the bride's long white
taffeta train—
               Not so fast! As our
clumsy protagonist hovers midair
above low clouds of dry ice and charmeuse,
double the hair spray, square off all the shoes:
it's 1989 in Isfahan.

: : : :

It's 1989 in Isfahan,
another bride and groom walk down the aisle
on a Naïni carpet and Cloud Nine:
my mother, young and doll-faced in a shawl
of lace and faux-pearl beading, a little shy;
my father with a twinkle in his eye
from the camera flash, sporting his ring
and a straight hairline still.
                      Two hands entwine
on the next page: her French acrylics clash
with his mechanic's nails, each worn half-moon

eclipsed with grease he's scrubbed with a wire brush
to no avail.
    And yet she's murmuring,
I do, I do. Now he may kiss the bride.
I wish I could have been there by their side.

      :   :   :   :

I wish I could have been there. By their side,
holding my father's arm, could that be him,
first love and friend, grandfather and guide—
I wish he could be here, where we call home . . .
Roused like a genie from the silver ring-
back tone back home, put him on speakerphone:
"Stop that kid from reading. He'll go blind."
Unhappy in his body, the kid's all mind,
or so he thinks, turning from life to books,
because he'll never get by on his looks?
He loves his mother and other boys too much,
and everything he says will come out botched.
Was it for this they abandoned everything
in the Islamic Republic of Iran?

      :   :   :   :

In the Islamic Republic of Iran,
we do not have such a phenomenon.
The West is stealing clouds from Persian skies.
Death to America! Militarize!
Close all the mosques, lock up all the prayers
in a No-Fly list to justify our wars.
My ill-matched countries, 'tis of you I sing
as bombs and rockets bursting on the air-
waves and our screens give proof to your common cause
that flags exist, that God is still out there
somewhere.
    Recast the self-fulfilling ring
Auden forecast Bin Laden by: that those
to whom evil is done, must do preemptive evil—
the nonsense palindrome whereby we live.

: : : :

The nonsense palindrome whereby we live
the future as already past, backward,
fooled even Shakespeare. No poet can redraw
or edit the tide of time almighty, no verse
reverse the flow or add to the reserve
of hours trickling through the cracks. But dear
reader, as we hang briefly on this thread,
I feel in my gut the tug of each dark line
made taut before it breaks against the nil
margin where all life goes. And so I'll loop
the unwinding tapes back onto the spool
of my one reel, my father's wedding ring,
admitting I was wrong, and with a grin
accept the future I've been given to live.

from *The Hopkins Review*

GREG DELANTY

To Our Indolent Cancer

◊ ◊ ◊

Ah, our lazy, our listless, our lovely, our lingering
languid turtle; mooching, smooching slow dancer;
dozy, dossing, easygoing footdragger; tinkering,
plod-plodding procrastinator; incipient necromancer;
lackadaisical, lackluster, loafing, lagging lug;
watched pot; fainéant of fainéants; otiose slug;

our break-taking, oscitant artisan slacker; our unfussed,
watching-the-grass-grow dawdler; our most phlegmatic
sloth; maundering, moony-loony manatee; nonplussed,
relaxed, dilatory, shell-slumbering snail; our aesthetic,
asthenic, torpid tortoise; lumbering Laodicean; dillydally-
ing, desultory lol-lol-lollygagger; our shillyshallshally

our dear-there-where cancer, hear our lull-lull-lullaby.
You can, sir, be kind, be gentle, be easy, no need to rush.
We still have loads, bags, oodles of time. Remember: I die,
you die. We're both here now, why the sudden push?

from *The New York Review of Books*

ABIGAIL DEMBO

The Travelers

◊ ◊ ◊

A woman slid money across a counter, and said, "I'd like to travel."
"Where would you like to go?" the agent asked as a train rumbled past.
"I want to go to the childhood my father talked about . . .
the brick house on the edge of the town and the edge of the forest.
I want to see the chickens pecking at silence, shoot the chicken-stealing foxes
when they come. Is this reasonable?" "Yes," the agent said, swiveled in his chair,
then walked across the white floor, closing the blinds on the spare,
almost German, industrial district. "Your train will arrive presently."
The woman took a seat in the waiting room while a gray-haired old woman
turned the knob on a black-and-white television, and a man sat beside a squeaking fan.
"Where are you going?" the younger woman asked them. "Where I can hear one strand
of Dvořák practiced on a piano in a basement—sit with my face between my knees
at the top of the stairs or press my ear against a vent in the floor," the man replied.
"Well," the older woman said, "this time I'll carry one finch in my hands like a cube
of ice from a house on fire. Last time, I ate green horehound in my bed at night,
and all day swept a candy store floor. My tongue was like a snake's.
My room was cold as a wharf." The old woman knocked soot off the arms
of a worn chair, turned the television to the weather station, restless
as a snowdrift, restless as the small bones, the drum of an inner ear.

from *Five Points*

JOSE HERNANDEZ DIAZ

My Kafka Prose Poem

◊ ◊ ◊

    I woke up and logged on to Twitter to discover someone impersonating me. They said I like to read novels in the bathtub, but I don't have the attention span for that, and, besides, I only take showers. They posted things with swagger instead of second-guessing and qualifying every thought like I do. They created another personality for me, one who doesn't feel guilty about going to Starbucks, Amazon, or other corporate chains: a carefree everyman, one could say.

    When I reported this to Twitter Support, they said I was the actual fraud, that my name didn't match my ID card. I told them that's because it's my pen name and my mother's maiden name as well. They told me to take a hike and get a real job because writing is a form of criminality. I now wander the damp streets looking for my past self. The one with 25K Twitter followers and a sense of purpose. Follow me, dear friends, beneath the scattered moonlight. I'm craving Starbucks, again, but the real me feels guilty about it.

from *The Southern Review*

TISHANI DOSHI

Egrets, While War

◇ ◇ ◇

In the garden, egrets are doing their stalking
dance, and it's easy to see how they are really
feathered dinosaurs flown in through a hole
from the past. Somewhere, a city under siege
remains sleepless. The dirge of *loss recovery*
loss loss loss   continues. I cannot say
why other people's family portraits fill me
with such tectonic longing. Ancestors
who stepped from ocean to land, shedding fin,
tail, gill, to transform into a symphony
of great-aunts and uncles. We bury clues
of our dispossession—bony-plated language,
heart scarab. Our task is to march on. To rise
and leave the apple orchard, throw stones
at marauders who threaten to tear up
the carpets. Father will file a missing person
report while spring carries on with its hedonism.
It is pointless to resist the pull of our fruiting
bodies. Whatever we fear has already happened.
Will keep happening. If we could just wake
to fullness in a delta with the berry-red lips
of an amorous god upon us. Climb trees
to listen to heartbeats. But here, the earth
remains leashed to mystery—clay fingerprint,
fragment of jaw. The sea retracts her tongue
like a warning. Winged creatures lurch
and soar. Whiteness, then vanishing.

from *Harvard Review*

DENISE DUHAMEL

Poem in Which This Fathead "Fat Ass" Admits It

◊ ◊ ◊

My then-husband told me a student told him I had a "fat ass." She was a great poet, a feminist, someone I'd been so happy to teach. Why would she say that? And why would she say that in front of him? *I don't know, but I wouldn't trust her*, he said. Why did I trust him? And why did I even care? Why wasn't I adult about it? I *did* have a fat ass. I *do* have a fat ass. Why didn't I simply let it go? Why was I such a fathead about my fat ass? Why, oh why, did I confront her? Why did I say *I thought you were a feminist. I can't believe you said that.* But apparently I did believe it. Why wasn't *I* more of a feminist? Why did I believe my husband over her? The student explained she'd said that I *kicked ass* which, of course, in context makes more sense. But I was already invested in my anger. I was a fat fathead ass. I didn't know yet my husband was a liar—this lie mild compared to the ones to come. Or I knew deep down in my fat gut, but the information hadn't yet reached my fat head. I did the worst thing possible—agreed to believe them both. As the student cried, I remained silent and stern. She dropped out of college—how could she continue when I was such a fat ass fathead? Shortly thereafter my fathead husband dropped out of our marriage. I hope this poem will make her feel slightly better. That my fat ass misery will make her chuckle and say, *what a fathead that professor was.*

from *DMQ Review*

ELAINE EQUI

Lorca's Guitar

◊ ◊ ◊

I saw it on display,
the case lined with red velvet,

like part of his body—his voice—
or a companion of his voice

laid out in an open casket
sealed within a glass box.

It was a small instrument,
almost a ukulele,

this skiff that carried him
across the lake of deep song.

I stood before it, listened,
and heard nothing.

No "wind in the olive trees,
wind in the mountains."

I thought it looked homesick, as the poet
himself had been homesick in New York.

I hope there is a museum guard,
some shy boy,

who comes when no one is around
and plays it.

from *Action, Spectacle*

GERALD FLEMING

Two Thousand

◊ ◊ ◊

One Sunday morning thirty years into their marriage, they made love. Soon one of them would get up & make coffee, but first they'd rest, and as was their habit, stare toward the ceiling quietly.
He mumbled something, and she couldn't make it out.
"What'd you say?"
"Oh, nothing."
"I thought I heard you say *two thousand*."
"Nah—just mumbling."
"You said *two thousand*, didn't you?"
"I guess I did. Two thousand."
"Two thousand what?"
"That's two thousand times we've made love since we got married."
"What? You've been *counting*?"
"Well, yeah. Sort of informally."
"There's no such thing as *informal counting*. Oh, my god."
Naked beside him, she went silent, and wondered what exactly constituted his *one* and what did not. And what else he'd been counting.
"What else have you been counting?"
"Don't ask," he said.
She thought their love was an elm with innumerable leaves, she thought their love was lilacs & a tangle of thorny roses, she thought their love a long bask in the complex sunlight of language, she thought their love difficult & brilliant, a spiral staircase, a thatched hut, a high window, a gesture, a lucky error, a mad, unexpected wind.

from *BODY*

JOANNA FUHRMAN

How to Change the Filter on the Developing Cell Matter in Your Womb

◊ ◊ ◊

If you wake up early, the genre is rom-com: the cells trade insults with a grad-student waitress with dimples.

If you microwave your frozen Pop-Tart, it's sci-fi. An alien beams up a fertilized egg so they can kibbitz about time travel.

If you double the shots in your Americano: action! A fetus drives a McLaren 720S into an amniotic sac.

If you choose to go back to bed—maybe mumblecore? You keep adjusting the womb's speaker, but still—you can't make out . . .

If you read the *New York Times* on your cell phone, it's clearly an Oscar winner. The sibling of the disabled fetus learns how to hide his tears at the truck-stop cervix.

If you read the back of the cereal box, it's a documentary. A talking head explains why the fetus isn't kicking.

If you throw the cereal box against the wall: French New Wave. The fetus's naked ass complicates the meta-dialogue about the commercialization of Hollywood film.

If you wear red lipstick under your KN-94, a musical is born. In glittery feathers, the mother's bladder tap-dances. The thin hairs on the fetus sway together Busby Berkeley–style, forming an arch, then spiraling into numerous rhinestone-adorned spokes.

If you cry in the driver's seat of your minivan: melodrama strikes! Once the fetus falls in love, his deadly illness is detected.

If you text your ex an inscrutable emoji—oh, the horror: the fetus attacks the host with dissonant chords.

If you take a selfie with your childhood stuffie: Studio Ghibli. The fetus morphs into a cat-shaped balloon and floats out of the womb.

If you walk to work, it's a costume drama. Each style of chapeau suggests a new stage in the fetus's psychological development.

If you skip work, it's film noir. It was all the dame's scheme. There never was a fetus in the womb.

from *The Georgia Review*

AMY GERSTLER

Postcard

◇ ◇ ◇

Thanks for the shoebox full of peyote buttons.
It arrived safely, though a bit roughed up
by the post office. That spineless little cactus
has advanced my narrative! Ingesting three
buttons per day makes me feel like less of
an afterthought, shoves me deeper in love
with whoever I meet. Yesterday, for example,
Lynn showed up in her jacket with the pink
velvet collar and I was quite beside myself,
as possessed by the living spirit of her thrift store
wrap as by her high-density self. So you see,
the peyote is obviously useful! Stories
are pouring out of me as storms through
a sieve. Tales I'd never had the heart
to tell, or in some cases even remember
are now being beamed back to me, albeit
forcibly, via vertiginous lightshows. I've
been practicing shrinking. Please return
home as soon as you graduate rehab.
That's fabulous the staff can't seem to tell
that most of you residents turn in kitten piss
for your drug tests. Sorry about the bedbugs.
Glad everyone got a new mattress. I miss
your renegade brain, your melodious,
jet-lagged laugh. Did you know the word "Peyote"
derives from the Nahuatl, from a root *peyōni*,
meaning "to glisten"? You've always glistened
indispensably. You and I were chasing something.
Come back. Let's see if we can catch it.

from *Revel*

JAMES ALLEN HALL

Inheritance at Corresponding Periods of Life, at Corresponding Seasons of the Year, as Limited by Sex

◊ ◊ ◊

Some species mate, then decapitate.
Some frogs never reproduce the same
place twice. Some species film with
fancy cameras their fucking. My father
said my mother requested one night
to be whipped by strangers. No species
lack pleasure receptors in their ears.
Some bees use sex as revenge, some
as memory. Fell ponies never uncouple.
Some sharks orgasm with their eyes
so can never trust their seeing. My father
said *I can't do it*, sent my brother inside
the porn store to buy what my mother
wanted. Some call out to a god, others
to excrement. I am not making equivalencies.
Finches sing to seduce. Ornithologists
theorize the same song also eulogizes
if produced in a tree hollow. That this is
not the saddest fact in all of zoology is
zoology's saddest fact. Unprompted,
my mother told me she loved my father
like a brother. Some mate for safety, to avoid
sadness, to self-flagellate. Some say *there,
there* as if pushing on a bruise. After

her affairs, my father forgave his wife.
For all species, desire is the most boring
verb, yet they connive for it most hours.
Some species of snake copulate in hopes
they are another species altogether. Grunion
bury their spawn in sand. My mother said
she would have aborted me, but the clinic
was closed. When whales abandon a grieving
mother, she does not find kindness again.
Some lives are taken down to salt, some to water.
Some species invent facts about the living
to explain the dead. I cannot fathom the bones
I find in the woods posed themselves like this,
though some species of grief find meaning
in minutia, a mechanism for survival. It is hard
to imagine a face for each skull.

from *The Adroit Journal* and *Poetry Daily*

JEFFREY HARRISON

Amnesia

◊ ◊ ◊

In my dream, someone mentioned
"Kenneth Koch's great poem 'Amnesia.'"
"I don't remember that one," I said,
but suddenly, as though projected on the air,
I could see the first few lines.

I decided to go home and find
the rest of the poem but couldn't remember
where home was. When I woke up,
of course I was home, but I didn't
remember those lines from the poem,

and when I looked through Kenneth's books
I didn't find a poem called "Amnesia"
or even "To Amnesia," one of his odes,
which might have begun, "I'm sorry I forgot
to write a poem about you / until now!"

Remembering that the internet
remembers everything (supposedly)
I googled "kenneth koch + amnesia"
and found a poem entitled "Amnesia"
in the online magazine *Jacket*

by the Australian poet John Kinsella
but *dedicated* to Kenneth Koch. Weird—
was I still dreaming? (No.)
I liked the poem but couldn't help thinking
it wasn't quite as much fun

as Kenneth Koch's "Amnesia" would be—
a poem that exists only in my dream
and wherever dreams go when you
wake up; a poem whose first few lines
I briefly knew but can't retrieve,

though I can picture him writing it
in his headlong scrawl, and I won't forget
that, in my dream, someone
(though I can't remember who)
called it great, unforgettable.

from *The Threepenny Review*

ROBERT HASS

A Sunset

◊ ◊ ◊

The sky tonight on the top of the ridge
Was bruise-colored, a yellow-brown
That is one definition of the word *sordid*,
And which, I think, used to describe
That color, carries neither a moral
Nor an aesthetic judgement. The sky
At dusk was sordid and then brightened
And softened to a glowing peach
Of brief but astonishing beauty,
If you happened to be paying attention.
I could take a hard right here
To the angry adolescent boy in Texas
Who shot and killed nineteen children
With a high-powered weapon my culture
Put into his hands. How to enter
The hive of that mind and undo what
The imagination had done there?
He bought body armor at a local store,
Two rifles; one of which fires forty rounds
A minute. He had it specifically in mind
To kill children of that age, the lithe-
Bodied young in their end-of-term clothing.
The connective tissue in this veering
Is the idea that it is the experience of beauty,
Not rules, not fear of consequences
Or reverence for authority, that informs
Our moral sense. This may be where
John Ashbery would introduce a non sequitur,

Not from aversion to responsibility,
But from a sense he no doubt had,
That there was a kind of self-importance
In the introduction of morality to poetry
And that one might, therefore, be better off
Practicing one's art in more or less
The spirit of the poor juggler in the story
Of Christmas who, having no gift to bring
To the infant god, crept into the church
In the night and faced the crèche and juggled.

Play, beauty, the impulse to reproduce it,
The impulse to evoke and bring to rage
And then to stillness the violence
In our natures. One does not,
The argument is, watch *Lear* and then
Go out and kill someone. The next veering,
Undertaken without cynicism, but
In a spirit of frankness (leaving aside
Plato's originary arguments) would be
To introduce the collection of records
They found in Adolf Hitler's bunker.
There were more than a hundred
Of them: Wagner, of course, the operas
Especially, but also Mussorgsky,
Rachmaninoff. He must have turned,
To rest his mind, from reports on the success
Of Zyklon B to the concertos of Rachmaninoff.
Monet might be the counter-argument.
I've read that, in his distress at hearing
Descriptions of the violence of the earlier war,
The mud and excrement and rotting bodies
And barbed wire, poison gas, the rows
On rows of young men hurled by their officers
At one another's cannons and machine guns,
He rose one morning, walked down to his studio
By the pond at Giverny and began
To paint the water lilies and kept painting them
As long as his hand could hold a brush.

It's late. I need to return to the subject
Of that boy's mind and the art we practice.
And the sunset—peach to dull gold which faded
To what felt, for just a second, for less
Than a second, a blessed and arriving silence,
And then a pale green at the skyline,
And then dark. And it was Monday night.

Plato's idea, I think, was that beauty
Was an ordering of elements the world offered
And that the harmonies in that order
Taught the soul the good. A later culture
Would say that boy was taken by a demon
And study ways to exorcise it. The devil
Had a name: it was the love of evil.
And us? Is there a practice of the arts
That would install, inform, would
Deeply root a culture that would form
A mind or heart in which those young bodies
On the classroom floor had become
Unimaginable, from a love of the good
As ordinary as the children's tennis shoes?
Probably not. Do we need to be able
To touch that mind? At that age?
It could have come from being laughed at.
Once. Or perhaps there was a sexual thrill
In putting on the costume, carrying
The rifle, saying I Am Doom as he strode
Across the parking lot. Is there a way
To undo the stew of computer games
And horror films and superhero fantasies
That gave a language to the moral injury
He wanted to inflict? Or the culture
Of resentment and fear that put the weapon
In his hands? Those people run governments.
Here's another hard right turn. Think
Of how Walt Whitman loved this country,
Loved the president who died. Imagined
Himself as a hand brushing a fly from the brow

Of a sleeping child. In the dark
I thought of a radiant ordinariness
That burned, that burned and burned.

from *The New Yorker*

BOB HICOK

The call to worship

◊ ◊ ◊

The possibility that the zero gave birth to the universe,
that all our somethings come from nothing, the fear
of being alone like that, children of chance, orphans
down to our atoms, is mother to the idea of god. God

is a dress we slip over solitude, a mask
for oblivion to wear, a rule-giver in a world
where no flower or bear cares that we are here
or what we do.

I prefer a theology of silence, the eschatology
of the shrug, a religion of holding my wife's hand
for now.

But if the industry of the church is what it took
to give me bells ringing Sunday mornings,
to which crows sometimes rise and deer turn,
I'm grateful for a sound that pulls me out of myself,
lifts my head toward sun and clouds, into the up
and all, the blue, the on and on of it, when I bend
the only knee I have to bend, feel
happily small, contingent, and held, by what
I can't say, short of everything.

from *The New Yorker*

NAZIFA ISLAM

The Wind Whipped Tears into My Eyes

◊ ◊ ◊

a found poem: The Unabridged Journals of Sylvia Plath

A softspoken God said he couldn't bear
looking at my stump of a soul—
that I was becoming something dark and bitter

and he felt wary
of the growing crowd of tearful stars in my eyes.

Then he pushed his body
against me and he touched his lips to mine.
It was not romantic or delightful;

it was something cold
that broke me. I am alone now—

an unassuming creature wading through a field
of yellow grass—and how
I remember breaking from that incurable kiss.

The white light in him blinked
and scurried, raveling around me.

from *The Southern Review* and *Verse Daily*

HENRY ISRAELI

Escape Artists

◊ ◊ ◊

Who remembers Tony Curtis as Harry Houdini immersing himself
upside-down into a tank of water in a straitjacket with a bundle of chains
wrapped around his chest only to emerge mere minutes
later to take a bow? The trick was there was no trick,
just skill and a hidden key—in his mouth, I think, although
my memory of it is hazy.
                         My father had to cover himself in leaves
and snow to blend into the forest ground which was his bed
for over a year. His uncle once lay dead
still beneath a plank under a bale of hay in his Polish girlfriend's barn,
and when the bayonet pierced his shoulder through straw and board,
kept completely silent.
                       What Jew hasn't, at one time or another,
had to become an escape artist? Harry Houdini, born Eric Weiss,
son of Rabbi Mayer Weisz, years earlier dropped the "z" to sound
less Jewish upon coming to America from Budapest.
Bernard Schwartz vanished behind Tony Curtis,
and starred in over a hundred films, including *Houdini* in 1953,
which ends with Harry pulled from a water tank,
dying from a ruptured appendix,
promising his wife "if there's any way, I'll come back"
because even he couldn't disappear forever.

from *The Massachusetts Review*

FATIMA JAFAR

In the End of the Beginning of Our Lives,

◊ ◊ ◊

we devoured all our hours together. In shimmering heat,
I slept on a mattress, a record scratching terrible music
in the back. I cut out shapes of letters from blue paper,
cut out stars, full stops, stuck them above my bed to
signify anything. Teenage bones, warm like a hunched palm,
belling against light. We knew everything then: sunsets,
sunrises, the charred chalk of winter mornings by the sea.
After class, brewing pots of green tea and watching movies,
we spun the worst parts of ourselves into false lives. School was
old, its checkered books and faint ink of bored ideas. Black shoes
devotedly filthy against Monday mornings, ready for the
pink work of our daily mythologies. In the forest of years,
we hunted for beauty, dug out of the dirt an older cousin's
tub of eyeliner, liquid glitter, a tube of graying gloss. Taught
ourselves, in bramble and in thorn, the slow art of decoration.
In mirrors, the easiest part of girlhood stood waiting, as brief
and delible as a new flower, begging, begging again, to be plucked.

from *The Kenyon Review*

BRIONNE JANAE

The Heart

◊ ◊ ◊

has many rooms   doors that open   doors
that don't   still a lock to pick   a key to find or borrow
or have carved by the right smith
some doors only open when another shuts
some never open   the locks red with rust and glazed
with spider's web   sometimes I think I want no doors only arches
or windows you have to scramble through when no one's watching
you might think it was but it's not a storage space   neither holding cell
nor jail   you have to let the light come and go as it pleases
the heart can't be bought or owned   it's terribly difficult
but not impossible to lose   sweet friend I found a room
inside my heart I think could suit you
a place I hope you will return   you can turn the fire on
or leave it cool   you can shut the shades or leave them open
write your poems on the wall or only lie on the floor dreaming

from *Allium, A Journal of Poetry & Prose*

RAPHAEL JENKINS

Two men too man to mourn

◊   ◊   ◊

> *All the books say that when your best friend's mama die,*
> *you ain't got no parents neither.*
> —Camonghne Felix

We are in Detroit, seven years ago,
hiding in my whip, two grown-ass men,
full-on ugly crying—all snotty.
We left da homie's momma's funeral
halfway into her eulogy, hearts too soft
to be seen, despite the bruising's cause
lying in a gold casket, in a sanctuary filled
with more bruised hearts. Bruh had a square to share.
We inhale prickly exhaust hoping for calmer nerves
that never come, thank God every hood church stands
around 200 feet from a liquor store. We don't break a sweat
click-clacking across the street in our wingtips to fetch some leaves
to roll gas, & our bottles of expected masculinity. We had no jokes
to trade for laughs, so we got slapped to keep from weeping as we
circled the block. Swerving back into the church parking lot
for the repast, we do not speak. Sloshing & swallowing the only sounds
as we swap swigs of brown smolder between puffs of flower.
This is how we man up. This is how we show love to our dearly departed,
by taking into ourselves that which would have brought shame
in their living. We make libation liberation to escape what calls us to mourn
in the most human ways: a salt-wet face, gushing like a ruptured dam,
no longer able to hold back the flood of sobs & spit. With all the griefs
sure to come, our livers won't survive this manhood long, but it's the only house

we have blueprints for. Full of whiskey's holy ghost, we walk
back into the church, right feet slowly turning into left ones. No elder questions
our wobbling or sour-mash sweat. One auntie, mascara mudsliding down
her cheeks, just nods knowingly, & then points us to the buffet. We make
our plates, eat the yardbird, sop the gravy & try our best to forget how to cry.

from *Indiana Review*

VIRGINIA KONCHAN

Miraculous

◊ ◊ ◊

Outside, the air is perfume sweet,
the sky suffused in motherly hues.
A rich tapestry called past tense
unfolds, like a scroll, before me:
the future beckons, then leaves.
But what's truly amazing is this:
I step into traffic and it swerves.
I drink poison and vomit it out.
I encounter people who desire
to kill me with their bare hands,
and several have tried, only to
find their weapons shattered,
their ways scattered and lost.
Blessed, the poor and lowly:
blessed are those who mourn.
Tell a dream, lose a reader, but
every day, I swear, I am reborn.
Every day I meet with an angel.
Some minister to me, tenderly:
others clean and dress my wounds.
Some make it rain, mysteriously:
a very few pierce me through
my heart with arrows made of
alabaster marble and pure gold.
You might think I'm freaking,
but I'm wide awake, like Job.
You may think I'm joking, but
I'm not prone to joke anymore.

Thy rod and staff, they comfort:
I abide, and in abiding, forbear.
What if grace holds me together?
What if heaven is what earth is for?

from *The Missouri Review*

VICTORIA KORNICK

Eileen

⬦ ⬦ ⬦

did not say *lawyer*. She said *attorney*, and more often, *litigator*,
a word I could not have defined precisely.

It reminded me of *alligator*. Her father, an alligator.
I didn't know that from this word grew another she loved: *litigious*,

which meant nothing to me, but rhymed with *religious*.
Even in private, he is very litigious, she said, and I imagined him at prayer.

Eileen believed kneeling was in itself the most powerful gesture. *Fall
on your knees*, she sang at Christmas time, unaccompanied, always

stopping before the second half of the line. *O hear the angel voices.*
Of course it was sexual. But it was also not insincere.

When Jane started having sex, she said, *It only gets worse—
how much you think about it.* We were sixteen, and I didn't believe it was possible

to think about sex more than I already did.
Jane said Eileen was a liar, though. *No one could really enjoy that.*

And how often she did it—as if it were nothing.
It's not like she's tripping in front of these boys, and landing on her knees.

Eileen's father told her he'd chosen her mother
over another woman because he preferred her fellatio.

It was unthinkable, to me, to hear this from one's father.
The word, too. Like *fallacious*, an SAT word: mistaken, as in a belief.

Eileen believed it was not possible to experience pleasure
without the complete surrender or seizure of power.

When Jane talked about it, she said, *giving head*.
I thought of Marie Antoinette's, rolling. Or John the Baptist's, on a platter.

All day at school, I imagined presenting my head to an alligator.
I pictured him devouring it. And Jane said, one day, I would think about this
   even more.

from *Copper Nickel*

MARIANNE KUNKEL

Apostate Abecedarian

⋄ ⋄ ⋄

A sociology professor told my cousin
Break a rule in a public setting.
Cappuccino in hand, my cousin plopped
down in the front pew of a Mormon chapel.
Everyone turned when she slurped.
Filthier than coffee, according to Mormon
gospel, is immodesty—
how my sister looked wearing pants
instead of a dress to church. Simple, silky
jade bell bottoms, and next thing she
knew, her husband was appointed bishop,
locking her into weeknights at church,
more casserole deliveries,
nine relatives flying in for her daughter's baptism.
Over my dead body, my sister
persisted, resisting the baptism after
quietly reading that the Mormon founder
raped his seven underage wives.
Seventeen years young, I left the church
too timidly—shoved my Book of Mormon
under my bed, ghosted old friends.
Voicing anger came later: I studied
Wollstonecraft and hooks, heard
X and Bikini Kill, bought a *When there are 9* t-shirt.
You who rage inside church walls, giving
zero fucks if it's polite, I worship you.

from *The Threepenny Review*

MICHAEL LALLY

DC 1972

◇ ◇ ◇

1.
Every day seems to set a precedent for me.
The first rough trade bar I go to, a term I
didn't even know only months ago, is like
a parody of a tough straight bar, only the
Johns treat the so-called ladies with what I
take as more sincerity. The transsexuals and
transvestites and visiting servicemen from the
bus station next door are far from liberated
in the way gay revolutionaries use that term
but I'm surprised at how comfortable I feel
around them all. I'm with Ted who, in his
pursuit of his black identity, is discovering
more and more married fathers among the
black men he's seeing on the down low.

2.
The first night I go to The Grill with Ed, I
feel like a star just walking through the door
as the entire room turns to look and obviously
likes what they see. I feel like a spy as well,
inside a world few people know. The bar's
on Wisconsin in the heart of Georgetown, and
I've passed it many times thinking nothing of
it, as I'm sure most straight people do. But in-
side are mostly men who this night are singing
along to AMERICAN PIE while waggling their
fingers, creating an atmosphere only a straight
man couldn't appreciate for its mixture of inno-
cence and hope in the face of such an obviously
hostile world and sometimes desperate life style.

3.
I initiate a conversation with a man for the first time in a gay bar, a broad faced friendly looking guy with a beautiful smile, part African-American, part Island-American, part everything, eventually asking if he wants to go outside to find some quiet. After walking around a while I get up the nerve to ask if he'd like to go back to my place. Lee's up when we get there. She's been asking why I never bring any of my gay male friends home with me but I still feel guilty. In my bedroom I try to be quiet, which is a disappointment cause I've learned from male lovers that sex doesn't have to be serious or even continuous, but a mixture of sensuality, talk, laughter, and even shouting and carrying on.

from *R&R*

DANUSHA LAMÉRIS

Second Sight

◊ ◊ ◊

Back then, it freaked my friends out I knew things
I had no way of knowing, like that the 680 would be
closed the next day, a trip to Tahoe cancelled.
Or how I called my boyfriend the night before the giant quake,
told him, *Something big is going to happen tomorrow*, and
when it hit, I was in the open field everyone else was running to,
watching at a distance as windows cracked, chunks of glass
falling to the ground. *What's next?* they'd ask, as if I'd know,
or as if knowing would do any good, the world still coming down
around us: children kidnapped from the corner store, poison
in the water, planes shot from the sky. So when I dreamt
my parents' house exploded, I hoped it was a metaphor,
but the next week a fire climbed the dry scrub
and torched the gas lines. My family got out but lost
almost everything: photographs, Christmas ornaments,
my grandmother's gold. Though the gift of seeing is
something I think I got from her, my mother's mother,
if such a thing can be passed down. A rogue strand of DNA,
slipped into the chain, a code for *Here's what's coming*,
for *Beware*. Useless, maybe. Or maybe the way our line
survived—a pantry full of extra stores, an escape route
cut through the underbrush, a knife at the ready.

from *The Adroit Journal*

HAILEY LEITHAUSER

Five Postcards

◊ ◊ ◊

Dear Doll-Face, I miss you & by miss I mean maul
in absentia (the hairy-fresh scent of your pillowcase,
one smutched & kaput, tossed cotton ball); My Dearest
& Only Flamingo, near here is an elegant Belle Époque
boîte, a crowded candle-dim room with a piano that you
should be in; Dear Where Did You Get To You Rascal,
I'm ill-content & I want you, desire like fire each precise,
acquiescent, curvilinear inch; and maybe Hello From
Down South, does the moon way up there still reveal
her shocked kisser over the peak of the torn garage roof
or how's about an ordinary Greetings You Plump &
Deciduous, Smirched Girly Girl, I'm getting worried
that I am debased and forsaken and, Oh yeah, postscript
On the white kitchen table each night lies an icy great
salver of oysters that are heartedly waiting to be your
whole world.

from *Innisfree Poetry Journal* and *32 Poems*

AMIT MAJMUDAR

Patronage

◊ ◊ ◊

O for the days of assassin-dispatching, cousin-poisoning
Renaissance dukes with an ear for beauty in ottava rima,
of big-spending cutthroat Borgias in papal regalia
willing to lavish blood-slick ducats on the fine arts,
kings with rotten teeth who hanged pickpockets from bridges
but paid their pet playwrights a living wage, sherbet-sipping
Sultans who shuttled between the harem and the mehfil,
O for my very own surveillance-state Caesar Augustus
asking only that every so often a stanza liken him to Jove,
O for a dissolute aesthetic Pasha, or a Medici who gets me,
or some Rilkean widow offering a rent-free seaside castle,

anything but this committee of rivals and fossils,
unpublishable judges with grudges in a coffee conclave
glancing at my heart like a passport handed over
at heaven's border, snug mediocrities with slovenly offices
deciding whether I am fit to have a future here, the light
from my unwritten books still light years in the distance
reaching me for now, though there's no way to tell
if they've blinked out already, making way for the tenured night.

from *32 Poems*

CHRIS MASON

Well Water

◇ ◇ ◇

Covid booster
headache nap
memory: Fever
age seven
dream endless
vertical lines,
t.v. test
pattern representing
time. Age
seventy, event
horizon finished
blooming, stories
pulled up
in bucket
from well
of forgetting.
Kid reads
me words
printed on
nickel. Siegfried
the Flying
Saucer says,
"Look There!"

from *Bruiser*

GREG McBRIDE

Know Thyself

◊ ◊ ◊

I'm an old man now, getting to know myself,
my marbles still neatly arranged, like my taws
and cat's eyes in Quaker Oats boxes Mother
saved for me. But this morning, scratching an itch,
I noticed that my wrist is tiny, tiny telling lies.
So I checked a leg—my mighty quadriceps,
which have powered my life of runs and matches,
so many steps—and was appalled. Now,
there have been hints of a certain smallness
since starting out at six pounds, but this
—what can only be called a boy-sized leg
flexing in a failing crop of white leg hair—
gave me a start. I'm ridiculous it seems.
Do others know? I think of fun with my wife
in bed when I'd whisper, "Go ahead,
cop a feel of my *massive thigh*" (always
italicized), and she'd ooh and ahh
while stroking my strong, bowed legs, my grandpa legs.
She was in on the joke, I only sort of. I've run
for miles, lifted weights, done squats, climbed
up and down stairs, but it seems I've been gilding
a miniature lily. It seems this self I've carried
through time and place has been poorly housed
all along. My advice to young people:
As you make your way through life, check now
and then to be sure you know who you are.
You may be smaller than you thought.

from *FotoSpecchio*

JILL McDONOUGH

What We Are For

◇ ◇ ◇

At the Stop & Shop I joke with the girl helping me
find the star anise that it looks like someone left her
a chicken bone on the shelf. *Oh, isn't that nice*, she laughs.
They wanted you to have a fun surprise, I tell her, tell
the checkout lady I love her turquoise sparkle nails,
the gallery assistant I love his sweater, it makes him look
like a fuzzy baby bee. *Have a good day*, we all call
to each other: *Have a good one, a good weekend, good night.*
In the endless self-service kiosk line at the post office before
Christmas I tell everyone ahead of me who tries to open
the self-service kiosk drop-off box that it is full. They have
to walk their packages over to the counter, enormous stacks
toppling on the far right. Now you know, too. The third time
I tell someone and they don't thank me, the lady cop in line
with me just shakes her head. *They could at least say thank you.*
When she says this the last guy says *Thank you.* I say *No problem.*
When he's gone me and the lady cop crack up. I live for this
shit. *Do you think he heard me?* the lady cop asks. *He 100%
heard you*, I tell her, *and you are doing the lord's work.* Later
after the wine store and the library I see her and her partner
by their cop car and she says *Hey! You following me?* And I
yell *Of course I'm fucking following you you're the nicest
lady cop in town!* She is delighted, her partner's confused;
TELL HIM! she laughs. *You're an angel of holiday politeness;
I'm sticking with you*, I tell her, love this so much, being able
to walk through the world making people briefly happy, me
here with them but also here inside what this dumb grief
is making, purpose built for all this ache and love and awe.

from *The Threepenny Review*

JOYELLE McSWEENEY

Death Styles 5/6/2021: Terminator 2, *Late Style*

◊   ◊   ◊

I want that green possibility
the gravidity of late style
pregnant with self-possession
to Spring me to the end of the plot
Meanwhile I dream of Iphigenia
and how many times that teen can drop
in her altar top
When my teens are doing nothing
they are doing dance moves off TikTok
their brainwaves altering
like the ones with wands
who wave the planes down
and meanwhile I blow too much
dough on the baby's summer
clothes. Oh
well, if he wears it just once*
(*in the grave), then it's worth it.
I say the secret thought
in my brain like a spark
It lays down and snuffs
in the mossbane of the earbone.
It dies a crib death.
Bring me my toy stethoscope. No,
I can detect nothing. Two beer cans
on a cord? No. Radio silence.
Come in. Do you read me. No.
Wish I was done

like the LA River, put to bed,
maybe light up again by moonlight.
As a teen I watched *Terminator 2*
about the mom so strong she hurled
an 18 wheeler sideways down the riverbed
to lift her teen
on the shockwave. It was the only way
she could reach him.
What would that look like now
if I had the right device, what angel
would answer the landline
of that bad idea if I went scrambling with a branch
up the dome of heaven
to scribble my bad vow.
VEIL OF ERROR. Poor sow,
born with all your eggs in your basket
wish I took better
care before I went rootling up the interior
all the husks up with my tusks,
stampling down the shells.
That's just arithmetic:
you have so much time and then you run out:
rain rains stops and losses, the soffit rots
& floods the roof. Call the roofer. Meanwhile,
one man's half-minotaur,
and so more man than ox, while the other's
half-bucentaur, so twice oxen.
When speaking of men
one half finds a way
to be bigger. The roofer
won't come. The state barge
goes rolling down the levee
with its balls between its wheels
for the Wedding of Venice
to the Sea. Wild flowers
in the burn plane
form a swoosh
you can see from space
while the wood runs out
in the crematoria.

You have to help them out.
You have to lift the state barge of Venice
in your mom-arms
and send it caroming
down the LA River
till it reaches the end of the plot.
Spring in flames, an 18 wheeler
& Iphigenia. The dead can't help you.
You have to help them out.

from *Lana Turner*

ANGE MLINKO

The Bougainvillea Line

◊ ◊ ◊

Driving south, I cross it—the intangible line
beyond which bougainvillea grows,
beyond which the land is flagrant.
It's not exact; there is no sign
as with a border, so everybody knows.
It doesn't waft to me; it's not even fragrant.

When I see the burning bush, alarm
feels like joy. Staring intently can't
sear the retina, yet to capture
the exactness of its hue, a swarm
of violet tones descants
in throes of blind rapture.

Fire here, fire there, a phoenix bent
to a wall: flames trimmed to the shape
of an arch or a carport. Still,
no emergency crews are present.
It maintains its delicate crêpe,
burning out with a petulant sizzle.

. . .

Éblouissant, it evokes elsewheres
whose ghosts aren't nourished,
because the lime-lit ground and sun
conspire to illumine human affairs.
Open porches are encouraged,
and dogtrots for ventilation.

Enjoy close quarters, enjoy your neighbors,
suggests the bougainvillea. Exchange
formulaic pleasantries with aplomb.
Visit every day your street of little stores,
one for bread, one for wine; the range
of choice is never cumbersome.

Building materials are solid. Tomatoes
smell pungent, taste sweet and acid.
Where the bougainvillea is, thyme
gets crushed underfoot and rosemary grows
starry flowers so small because it is tacit
in its allegiance to the sublime.

The government is far away. It has always
been distant and corrupt, its fuss
just a radio signal, as night turns blue
and soirées in whitewashed houses blaze.
Dissolving clouds are amorous
as rained-on ink of billets-doux.

from *The American Scholar*

NICHOLAS MONTEMARANO

A Neighborly Day in This Beautywood

◊ ◊ ◊

Please pray for the. Kid on a bicycle
flipped and was lying. At all costs avoid.
Hello neighbors I propose we play.
Has anyone received a letter like this. We had
a sinkhole open. Here is a photo of a man
stealing our. What are you supposed to do when.
Sorry I ever posted anything about. Hey ladies
want to skinny dip with my manly self.
To the man walking his dog who took a picture
of my. Not looking for a debate. Update
he has passed and has been picked up.
To those with children be on the lookout for.
Not a single squirrel left. Due to an expecting
baby. I've been hearing helicopters.
To the person who called the police on me.
Before you get into an argument with some
rando. More proof bad people will conspire.
Our food stamps didn't come due to. Hi everyone
you may remember back in October my husband
was killed. If these are your kids let them know.
Whoever is setting off fireworks please
stop. Always check your food before opening.
Man wearing red baseball hat dancing
and swearing. What on God's green earth.
Beware. Now for a true story. Getting married
in a few weeks. Looking for a getaway car.

from *Copper Nickel*

_# YEHOSHUA NOVEMBER

What About the Here and Now?

◊ ◊ ◊

"When you die, you will meet God,"
reads the billboard
foregrounding the stretch of industrial factories
off the state highway
on my commute home each night.

★

When I was twenty-four,
I felt a great weight lift
as I walked past New Life Dry Cleaners,
Squirrel Hill snowmelt underfoot,
and first believed
in the Baal Shem Tov's conception
of Divine Providence:
Each leaf's falling,
each turn on the way down,
is prefigured in—at each moment,
governed by—
the Divine imagination.

★

The next week, a faceless force pulled me
out of my chair in the star poet's course
on Apollinaire and the French Surrealists
and placed me in a New Jersey yeshiva.

In the study hall, a rabbi, thin as a reed,
translated a Chassidic discourse
on the world's nonexistence:
Creation relative to the Ein Sof
is like a sunray inside the globe of the sun itself.
Because everything transpires within the Divine,
nothing occurs
that is not fated.
I sat motionless in my seat
for thirteen months.

*

Once, after the day's last prayers,
I was summoned to the payphone
in the run-down yeshiva coat closet—
rabbinical students' dusty fedoras hanging on hooks—
to hear my dark-haired wife whisper
she was pregnant
with our second child,
our first son.

*

A week before his birth,
in need of employment,
I crossed the bridge that led to Brooklyn,
mythic city of my father's childhood,
to discuss *The Metamorphosis* with twenty-year-old
seminary students just returned
from the Holy Land,
who, I suspected, would take issue with
their Czechoslovakian brother's modernist conviction
a million random factors
had come together just so
to bury his life.

*

Kafka passed away
on the First of Sivan,
anniversary of the Jewish nation's arrival
at Mount Sinai—
the day, the midrash states,
all theological debates were set aside,
and two million Jews camped in the desert
like one man, with one heart.

★

The roles and faces here are unrehearsed,
Szymborska wrote.
Still, in my nineteenth year, I spotted my intended
carrying a tray of steaming green beans
to the serving station on our first kosher kitchen shift
at the Upstate public university.
Thin arched eyebrows,
long dark hair,
a space between her front teeth,
eyes backlit by a calm radiance
I could not name.

★

Kafka's paternal grandfather, Yaakov,
was a shochet, a ritual butcher—
one who must possess exemplary fear of Heaven—
in the Czech village of Osek.
He believed in Divine Providence—
the force that stripped me from my table
in the yeshiva study hall
to explain to strangers of the opposite sex
at the Jewish night college
why an insect, once a man,
might climb a wall and cling to a photograph
of a woman in a fur coat,
cut from a glossy magazine.

★

We walk down a lane
between a corn-feed factory and a grassy field
in Postville, Iowa.
It is father-son weekend at yeshiva,
my eldest son's third high school
in three years.
At this one, the rabbis tell me
he is a good bachur, a serious student.
When I share this with him,
he looks down at the concrete path in disbelief.
When he was a boy,
I lost my temper whenever he stared off
during morning prayers, pushing away
a God I told him was close.

★

Before he was revealed
as the century's great mystic,
founder of the Chassidic movement,
the Baal Shem Tov,
known for his infinite patience,
served as a teacher's assistant in a Polish village,
walking the youngest children
to school and back.

★

Once, when I sat beside him
during evening prayers, my father,
away most nights at the hospital,
lovingly circled his thumb
around the back of my neck.

★

Kafka's mother gave birth to six children,
Franz the eldest.
Two brothers, Georg and Heinrich,
died before he was seven.
His three sisters, Gabriele, Valerie, and Ottla,
were murdered in the Holocaust.
Those who believe a Divine force
oversees every detail
are asked to explain the world's sadness,
but they can't.

    from *TriQuarterly*

SHARON OLDS

Health-Food Panties

◊ ◊ ◊

You could still drive—at the end of the weekend
you took me to the bus by way of the drugstore for a
refill for pain—no more chemo!
Goodbye, fuckin chemo!—it was hard for you
to climb back into the truck, but at the
health-food store we parked out front, I
stood by your open door, waving
the cars on by, as you slow slid down.
We browsed the aisles, mated for life,
I got some nuts for the bus and train,
your beautiful heavy face frowned and you
said, *"I'm covering this."*
We both knew that you liked that I always
wanted to pay my way, but that day
I added a couple of pairs of organic
cotton bikinis—one aqua, with smiling
rubber ducks, one pink, with apple
cider donuts with rose-colored frosting.
I would wear them when I'd visit you,
when you could no longer walk, or sit up, but I
would not mention it, we had our honor, which was
90% eros. I am looking at my ducks and donuts
now, my darling. You never got so you
could not kiss. And then you died. So I'm
kissing them now for you.

from *Prairie Schooner*

MICHAEL ONDAATJE

November

◊ ◊ ◊

Where is my dear sixteen-year-old cat
I wish to carry upstairs in my arms
looking up at me and thinking
be careful, dear human

Sixteen years. How many days since
I found you as if an urchin in a snowstorm

and you moved in assured
learned the territories of the house
and what became your garden

Only now do we see the horizon
where you paused two or three times
then slipped into

Was is too soon or too late
that last summer of your life
when we watched your walk
down to a river to take a sip
from its ongoing flow

Oh Jack I miss your presence everywhere
in the corners of rooms, in every chair,
or nesting in a cardboard box

Take me back where the past can again enter
those early remembered rooms, our snowbound street,
lift me upside down in your arms, I cannot stand it

I need a journey too. Have I slept my life away,
do I understand anything? Will I wear a bell
like yours into the afterlife where language
no longer exists and we gather only linked sounds
like oars from a passing boat,
those few syllables
to recall tenderness

You no longer wait for us

All day long, Bashō wrote,
A lark sings in the air
Yet he seems to have had
Not quite his fill

from *The Threepenny Review*

PÁDRAIG Ó TUAMA

Do You Believe in God?

◊ ◊ ◊

I accepted it for far too long,
lay down, said yes, said Anything you want,
said I'll follow.

                            I took that path, learnt all the rules.
                                 I was told I was a natural.
                                   I begged graces from a you.

It ended.
With a word. What word?
I don't remember.

                       Some voice said, Here's a map, drive off it.
                             When do I come back? I asked.
                                  You don't, it said.

Here's a road, a sleeping bag, a stove, a little bit to eat, it said,
and a night of stars, a fox along the border, a buzzard in the sky.
A hare whose speed you'll need.

                    Here's more grief. And sorrow. And a book. And
                                a number for a friend.
                                      Leave tomorrow.

I tried anything
I could get my hands on.
I dreamt of different endings.

> I paused instead of searching for the way.
> I found nothing and nothing
> never felt so good.

I return sometimes. Sometimes I like it.
I like the smells, the psalms, the bells for prayer
at midday and at six,

> the feeling of the beads between my fingers,
> the touch of skin to lips when someone
> puts a story in my mouth.

from *Alaska Quarterly Review*

JOSE PADUA

Godzilla Meets the Beast

◊ ◊ ◊

In some desert, yeah, I too came upon a beast eating its heart and I said, "Dude, what the fuck?" but in Japanese, and he said, in English, because the beast is white and originally from Pennsylvania, and because bilingual communication is common amongst us scary monsters, "I eat it because it is bitter, and because it's my fucking breakfast, ASSHOLE"—which made me reconsider all my previous assumptions about beasts, the lives they lead, and their proclivity for feasting upon their own vital organs. That's when snow started falling upon desert sand, that's when women wearing blue bikinis started twerking until they began to glow, and men wearing black boxer shorts ran frantically the fuck away from me. Tonight, snow will extend to the outer suburbs, leaving moist angels upon neon signs, a lovely cloak of fractals for the cold monuments of capitalism because I am Godzilla, King of Monsters, and we're all runaways on this planet, refugees from hideous demons and nefarious demagogues, waiting for the right cult to take us in, feed us cake, clothe us in delicate robes, tell us we're beautiful.

from *The Brooklyn Rail*

ELISE PASCHEN

After Killers of the Flower Moon

⋄ ⋄ ⋄

Lily Gladstone confides she wore my great
grandmother Eliza's blankets in three scenes.

I don't remember my great grandmother, though
in a photo, aged ninety, she holds me in her arms.

The actress plays Mollie Burkhart, who lived
down the street from Eliza in Fairfax.

Hands out wide, Lily says Eliza had a *broad wingspan*.
She pleated the wool broadcloth several times.

Through an open window, wings outstretched, an eagle
owl looms toward Mollie's mother, dying from poison.

My mother told me that owls in trees wailed
the windswept night before her father died.

Wrapping my great grandmother's striped blanket
around her shoulders, Mollie asks her husband,

during a downpour, not to close the window.
Be still, she says, and listen to the rain.

Eliza's blankets fold and unfold stories.
Into every pattern, I fly back home.

The Osage replaced hide robes with Dutch-
traded blankets in the mid-19th century.

I stop breathing during the night of film
when a murderer calls Osage women *blankets*.

While her husband injects Mollie with arsenic,
each sister is shot, poisoned, or bombed to death.

A woman, in a voice-over, foreshadows,
this blanket is a target on our backs.

In the quiet, after Mollie's obituary
is reported, I only hear rain.

Outside the theater, silent thunderbirds
overhead spread dark cloud-spattered wings,

outlining circles across a broadcloth.
Inside each target, a hole in the sky.

from *Poetry*

ALISON PELEGRIN

Zero Bothers Given

◊ ◊ ◊

     At last I have reached the perfect age,
which is my-tramp-stamp-needs-a-footnote
     years old. I have circled back, entering
a sort of informed childhood, a place where
     I can let my fat overflow and wear running shoes

     with dresses while relishing my newest moniker,
not MILF, but Woman of a Certain Age, woman
     abandoned by decorum who voices beliefs
and pet peeves so deeply tamped down
     their release is almost sexual: all lap dogs

     get on my nerves, today's students whine
too much, and to hell with high fantasy,
     The Hobbit most of all. I can finally say
to the Mystic Krewe of Mansplainers
     and the flag-happy truckers in this molon labe

     wonderland: *No one's treading on you, sweetie.*
And even though putting it in a poem
     is barely saying it at all, I feel brave,
and sort of emboldened, and I wish
     I had started sooner so there might be

     a spot for me in the Zero Bothers Hall of Fame
alongside that woman at Walmart who caged
     her own fit-pitching child with an inverted
shopping cart. Chaucer knew the sensation
     of yodeling down the mountain on the shorter

              side of days—*The lyf so short, the craft*
so long to lerne. Let the world be what it is,
              a dumpster fire, where robots write the poems.
As for me, moody grande dame of fickle tastes,
              I demand that my chain letter to the world

              be forwarded to as many people as possible
before it self-destructs. Before I do. I'm cranky
              already, stitching curse words in silk, shimmering
proof of my ill will. It won't take much—
              a pinprick would do it—to send me over the edge.

      from *The Southern Review*

DONALD PLATT

Streak

◊ ◊ ◊

        A jackknifed semi full
of dried feed corn has spilled its whole cargo over the eastbound lane
           of State Route 231.

Driving the other way, I find myself humming along with Mitzi Gaynor
           cartwheeling in *South Pacific*,
"I'm as corny as Kansas in August . . ." Across the median, the highway

           has become golden
dunes of pebbly sand that men in green vests with diagonal, silver
           reflective stripes

shovel toward a white truck's black, swaying, elephant-trunk-like
           proboscis sucking all
that bounty up. I hear Gaynor keep singing, "I'm as normal as blueberry pie . . .

        I'm in love,
I'm in love with a wonderful guy." That ecstatic show tune makes me
           remember all

those gangly guys I had a half-unconscious crush on, with long
           or short cocks and hairy balls,
doing the hundred-yard dash naked across the lacrosse field at halftime

           in 1974, April of my junior
year in high school. The streaker craze. Vietnam and Watergate.
           I was humming, "I'm as horny

as bucks in the springtime . . ." At the Oscars that spring, a man with long
    brown hair and bushy
mustache streaked across the stage behind actor David Niven,

   who was introducing
Elizabeth Taylor to open the envelope for Best Picture.
   As he was saying,

"A very important contributor to world entertainment . . . ," the streaker
    jogged out from the wings,
grinning and flashing a peace sign. The agile film editor,

   who had thirty seconds
of delay time on the live broadcast, managed to show only the streaker's
    slim torso, no genitals

except for the initial split second where you can still catch a fleeting
    glimpse on YouTube
of his thick, dark pubic hair. Niven fidgeted with his black bow tie,

    shrugged, couldn't help
laughing with the audience. He interlaced his fingers—"Well, ladies
    and gentlemen, that

was almost bound to happen. But isn't it fascinating . . ." The audience,
    which had momentarily
quieted, began tittering again. Niven pulled at his left earlobe,

    formulating
his famous, impromptu line—"Fascinating to think that probably
    the only laugh

that man will ever get in his life is by stripping off and showing
    his shortcomings."
The crowd exploded, started clapping. Niven smiled

    drily in the English
manner. "Now, if I might continue with the introduction . . ."
    and Elizabeth Taylor

swept in, making her grand entrance, tanned, in a low-cut yellow gown,
gardenias in her hair.
Her earrings, drooping loops of diamonds. She began, "That's a pretty

hard act to follow . . ."
Living is a pretty hard act to follow. We are naked men and women,
exposing our shortcomings,

running for three seconds of fame across a stage. His name was
Robert Opel.
He became a gay rights activist and gallery owner in San Francisco.

A year after Nixon
resigned, he campaigned for President "on a platform of complete
disclosure."

At his first press conference, he naturally appeared naked and said,
"I've got nothing
to hide." His campaign slogan was *Not Just Another*

Crooked Dick.
He was shot and killed in an attempted robbery by two men
strung out on speed.

As Gaynor sings it, they were "high as a flag on the Fourth of July."
Our lives are corny.
So much spilled grain. A single golden streak across a highway.

from *Plume*

JANA PRIKRYL

The Channel

◊ ◊ ◊

> GLOUCESTER: There is part of a Power already footed...
> —*King Lear*, 3.3.13

Through mildewed windshield of the bridge my France
and I can see the cliffs begin to show
the more as night approaches. Particulates
that dim the glass release what glows to warmer
glowing. In-betweens like this we had
at every stage, and neither had to tell
the other the light falling is rising.

We double-checked the list of things to do.
Together made a plan to steer some beaches
west of Dover, land in darkness, darkness
in that century a toothèd beast that we
will yoke, march our men back east and there
when he remembered, in the middle
of our planning as if planning freed him

to remember something left imperfect
like the stove on or the bathroom light
which imports so much fear and danger
his personal return was most required
and necessary. It has been asked, know you
no reason the king of France so suddenly
is gone back? The matter made explicit,

proxy for my own repeated asking
though some assume that France remained in France
when I sailed north, neglecting the small
wrinkle in the fabric: he came along
and then he turned around, which may be worse?
I tell myself it is a privilege
to hear my thoughts run out against my will

and few events on earth can bring you here,
the very rim, where who you are goes on
into the sheer new time and voyages
without you since you watch her go, become
the parting of the two. The air between.
His self-awareness must have taken forms
quite painful. Recently eating an apple

the thought like stop-motion innocence ripened
all at once in me that he ate apples
and for a moment the inside of my mouth
was his. Last night it dawned on me: he slept
and nearly laughed. If he slept he woke, he
experienced morning. The list is long
of human things we almost did together,

the man I'd bring my famous cruxes to
though I'm afraid I know what he would say.
Rewrite, rewrite! Humans are the animals
with speech who let all of his manuscripts
go poof. It's wrong to make so personal
a mind so free, you say, but as he said
of overdoing things, it's fine for me.

France's lifeboat going down, I stood
looking like myself to starboard best
I could, at him till he had melted from
the smallness of a gnat to air and then
have turned mine eye and wept, alone
now in the plural sense of leading men
whose leader never speaks, Monsieur La Far.

They're joking over their pints and I nearly
expire, unused to marching although
nineteen and they on into middle age,
a sort of bonding drill beside a pub
by a canal. I hear again the cut
of Hazel's laugh when someone asked my plan
at university, take English, learn

everything, I said, quite literally.
Perhaps the only one who heard me right,
La Far's transplanted English wife who'd seen
some victories and knew what they were worth,
she laughed without much kindness in her voice
which did make me see myself as the child
I was. I smiled, every inch aware

how simple yet meant it more for that, to read
the landscape fore and aft, to read what's not,
the streams up to their sources and the roads
just hearsay in the place where I was born,
a distant bell, as though a small neglect
could be repaired, as if understanding
made up for failure to experience,

as if failure itself were a deeper form
of experience and there we stood at dawn,
Monsieur La Far and I, halfheartedly
suppressing what we knew the other knew.
A croft of trees advanced from down the hill,
a flight of ravens circled overhead,
we read the signals as two readers will,

interpretation so intrinsically
equivocal when there is only one thing
you can do. Who can tell me how event
touches on the next event, what substance
forms the point of contact, where connects
enlarges every time you read the text
when I remember certain books I haven't

and now wish I had despite their dullness
thoughtless English, drafty construction
and had to ask, my captain, taste, the ear,
my sense of what is good, could it be
a style of selfishness permitting me
to use the shipping lanes the careless use
who think about themselves from first to last

from *The Paris Review*

ELIZABETH ROBINSON

The Extinct World

◊ ◊ ◊

We tried to explain the commonplaces of our childhood, but
their faces were dubious, concerned.

The transformation of a tadpole into a frog.

The smell of cut grass, we said, at which they looked down
to the dead soil.

We told them of the sequoia—a tree—so large a car could
drive through a portal cut through its base. The tree

—implausible—but "car"?

They were as aliens to us, yet we went on

to describe the sensuous pleasure of watching
a bee enter the cup of a flower and come out covered
with gold dust.

And honey, which we tried to demonstrate with polished
pieces of amber.

> We wished to extinct our grief, but grief was the one thing
> in endless supply.

We told them of sweetness, so many sweetnesses,
of a dark substance called chocolate that melted creamy

on the tongue, and the fleshy skin of bananas which
peeled away to reveal a white arc of fruit.

They were not ours, these ones who could not remember what no longer existed.

We prohibited the word "good-bye" because it carried the taint of redundancy.

from *Lana Turner*

MATTHEW ROHRER

Nature Poem about Flowers

◊ ◊ ◊

Looking back at photographs
our clothes were enormous draped
across our shoulders hanging
low off our hips like they were
someone else's and they were
usually someone's old flannel
it is clear we didn't care
or that we had different goals
for our clothes I remember
one night at the National
Arts Club B. seemed truly shocked
he said I always pegged you
as kind of a bohemian
but look at you in that suit
it wasn't unexpected
I drifted through the reading
nursing some very old wounds
acting like I was paying
attention there was somewhere
else I was dreaming about
the dappled and shifting light
of a forest in a book
where the air was cool and smelled
like imaginary flowers
and then we were applauding
and outside on the sidewalk
the city trembled and glowed
and we all felt it beckon
when F. pulled a purple chunk

of opium from his vest
at the bottom of tall streets
at Union Square a flowery
veil descended this was when
the city would wink at us
like it liked us or I thought
approved of us and when
we went to the movies
the actors were dressed like us
and one night it was the night
before I quit a lousy job
I had to get up and walk
it off and when I looked down
at my clothes under a streetlight
I saw they were all brown
everything I was wearing
and I heard the phrase glad rags
said by someone else
inside my head but also
I remembered the grown-ups
used to talk under their breath
about one of the older
kids how there was something wrong
with him it was obvious
because he only wore brown
and the elders nodded yes
the elders nodded wisely
and I guess I didn't care
because all in brown I stepped
out onto the avenue
—where spring sounded its high notes
and the blue air was perfumed
by all the flowering trees
that people who don't live here
don't believe in, the dogwoods
the redbuds, magnolias
—and I sneezed
and the avenue was lit up
like the deck of a ship
in the morning I would quit

my demeaning job but first
where the electricity
flowed unimpeded I too
wished to flow in my glad rags
through the streets of flowering
night and when I returned home
all the rooms were dark and S.
seemed asleep I quietly
slipped out of my enormous
shapeless clothes and opened
an ancient book trying once
again but without success
to live inside it never
coming out except at night
to finally persuade S.
that we could survive that way
that we could live forever
inside of books and she said
she could agree to part-time
and I said fine and we both
returned to the dreamy dark
that surrounds us but that
we don't share with anyone
and I dreamed I quit my job
by waving a sunflower
at my boss who had no power
over the natural world
and when I woke up I thought
that's not a dream that's just true

from *The American Poetry Review*

MARGARET ROSS

Cooperative

◊ ◊ ◊

The co-op board
conducts its monthly meeting.

Should they buy a golden luggage cart
to help with heavy packages?

No, no golden cart. It sends
the wrong message.

Can residents who paint or draw
display art in the lobby?

No, their art might be ugly.
And now comes Martin Adler

to explain he shouldn't pay
for the garage, the regulations

only mention rent from tenants
who use parking spots for cars.

What he parks is a trike.
He met his wife in the laundry room,

used too much detergent, suds
puffed up from the machine beside hers.

The new tenants resent the old
who paid so little all their lives

and now their only assets are apartments
they can't afford to leave. It creates

all sorts of problems says Dolores Reed.
The doormen have to check on them

and bring them medicine.
Skinny Mr. Weisz turns slowly orange

on his carrot diet, sitting in his loose beige suit
and rain hat in the lobby, he nods

at anyone going out, anyone
returning. His friend is Mr. Lee

the pharmacist in 7R, they sit together
sometimes on weekends.

On Halloween the children dare each other
to approach the Adlers' door

behind which Martin in an eyepatch
beckons from the haunted foyer.

It's a generous thing he does, some say
the only generous thing. He doesn't give

the doormen cash at Christmas.
The new tenants do. They send

their children to private schools
that teach the students they have made

the world more equal by contributing
their parents' pocket change to a penny drive

for the hungry. A hungry family
will receive a salad bowl of coins.

Why are they hungry?
Where is their money?

What if they told somebody at the store?
Carl, Larry, Angelo, Felipe,

or John attend the lobby, opening
and closing, questioning visitors, humoring

the lonely lobby sitters, in the slow hours
plugging in a tiny portable TV beside

the big TV playing its endless silent movie
of the alley and the driveway.

This is the night, the early early
morning when the tenants are locked inside

their dark apartments. Little poison houses
for the roaches tucked in corners

where a guest won't notice.
Larry's on. He might go

lie down in the basement
after mopping the lobby floor. And if anyone

wants in, they can buzz and wait.
Two exquisite dragons lace his forearms, one

for each child. The baby's dragon
breathing fire. It's begun to snow.

Orange snow lit by sodium vapor.
Pigeons huddle between details

on the carved facade. The limestone maidens
with their tragic postures.

Agony of the hand over the brow
beside agony of the hand pressed

to the cheek. On New Year's Mr. Lee
gives Mr. Weisz the pills he needs

to die in his bath and the water
runs over, seeping through the kitchen

ceiling of the Reeds. It was so traumatic!
says Dolores, just as friends were arriving

for dinner the plaster started crumbling. Gray chunks
all over hors d'oeuvres on the counter.

Upstairs, Angelo in the almost opaque steam
pulled Mr. Weisz up by the armpits

and held the dead man's torso
above water with one hand so the other

could turn the faucet off and yank the plug
and get the window open.

Cold on his skin.
And the street from up there—

not the salted pavement trudged by bundled figures
but a span of air maintaining distance

between buildings. Their various lights
where things were going on in rooms.

On a roof, the round medieval hut
of a water tower.

Somebody standing at the roof's edge
lighting firecrackers.

from The Paris Review

JAVIER SANDOVAL

Uncle Peyote

◊ ◊ ◊

Mexican cactus-squash of spiritual
whispers: my borderland brothers
    chew it like holy bread
    to quit other drugs,

but I take Peyote
to help me quit
    Peyote.

The shaman hocking it to me
over Venmo
    says it'll work eventually.
    Shaman—that's the title
    my unemployed uncle
    prefers.

Told me, Peyote
shows you nothing's real.
    Not you. Not me. Not
    even the need to work hard.
    My landlord's an illusion.

Told me, Everything
is just chemicals in your brain.
    Everything you see and feel:
    chemicals.
    The rush of a job well done:
    serotonin.
    The trust of a loyal friend:
    dopamine.

Told me, Love
is just the cocaine
      of poor people.

Told me, If helping old ladies
cross the street
      caused as many chemicals
      as the most innocent
      bump of pure, strangers
      would knock on strangers' doors
      asking for any grannies
      to stroll.

Told me, We'll only truly
believe in Love
      when we can
      buy it.

In my palms: this thorn-
crowned truth.
      I raise it, cupped,
      to my lips, trembling
      again into its dark church
      of forked tongues, black skies, stars
      we'll never reach till they

crater us; of we collapsed suns
devouring ourselves
      by swallowing what's
      small, yet infinite.

      from *Indiana Review*

EMILY SCHULTEN

Nocturnal

◇ ◇ ◇

We'd only just begun to scratch the floors
with our own furniture, unfold the box flaps

and hang the walls to look like our walls
in the old apartment: familiar faces, fruits.

Then we heard it, the long scrapes in deep
grooves overhead. It came from the devil's

peak, after we'd turned the bedroom into the same
dark as the night, but our eyes shone moons until

morning, afraid they might find a way loose, inside.
The exterminator said *rats*, and we patched a hole

with aluminum where the electric cable tightroped
from tree to tree past the roof. Still, they came back

at dark every day. My belly swelled with the life inside,
I wrenched the wrap of the sheet loose from its tuck

in the bed, and we heard the traps snap and drag
over us along the tracks worn in the wood.

The young pest control fella—only a child, really—
appeared each week, saw my middle grow fat

and bare feet swell in the door frame, leaned
his ladder against the ridge of the roof. It ended

in the summer, scorching. He climbed down
with a bulbous white trash bag, like a clump

of sugar apples dangling from his wrist.
(*Was it moving?*) Giddy, he explained his prize:

he'd caught three, as big as footballs. (His hands
held out to me an invisible canary melon.)

But more, actually, *I found one huddled in
the groove, tail snagged where the roof meets the house,*

pregnant. He grinned and walked to the trash.
I touched my stomach where I felt it kick

from inside. That night, the bed was quiet
and warm, the sheets soft and circling

our skin, the fan whished, and we stared
at the ceiling, at nothing, through the night.

        from *Ploughshares*

JANE SHORE

I Am Sick of Reading Poems about Paintings by Vermeer

◊ ◊ ◊

It used to be that you rarely saw a poem about a painting by Vermeer.
He could have been your long-lost Dutch uncle
twice removed in the days before those twenty-one Vermeers
migrated from Vienna, Paris, and The Hague,
a secret armada traveling by sea, by land, and air.
Four of them housed in the National Gallery's permanent collection
were hand carried down the back stairs
to join the month-long Vermeer reunion,
tickets more precious than the Super Bowl's.

Waiting for hours in the snow,
funneled twenty to a group, deposited four deep,
Vermeer-lovers nudged aside Vermeer-hoggers
who stared longer than the Vermeer-polite-viewing-time allowed.
Exiting the gallery, you could not reenter it,
but Vermeer-bereft-viewers could traipse upstairs to the empty
gallery of the contemporaries of Vermeer,
whose names sounded like you were gargling,
and who painted scenes of hair-washing and cooking, sleepy barmaids,
and pickpockets bilking passed-out cavaliers . . .

In the packed galleries of the Vermeers, the mood was festive,
courteous, hushed. It was a summit conference
of Vermeer-VIPs: museum guards whispered
into walkie-talkies, and scanned the crowds for Vermeer-violators—
paintings accidentally touched by some nearsighted senior's index finger
that got too close, but not, thank God,
like that crazed madman in 1972, who attacked

Michelangelo's *Pietà* with a chisel
(she lost a piece of her nose forever).

In the months following the exhibition, there proliferated
poems about Vermeer, Vermeer postcards and notebooks
and tote bags, facsimiles of pale girls and women
wearing a red hat or blue turban, women holding a flute
or reading a love letter or pouring milk or weighing gold coins
as they multiplied on coasters, on posters,
on note cards; *Girl with a Pearl Earring* gazed up at you
from the bottom of your mug at your last swallow of coffee;
her face undulating from scarves, on open umbrellas,
her cheek pecked by raindrops.

And there's my friend who spread *The Milkmaid*
chopped up into 2,000 jigsaw puzzle pieces
all over her dining room table.
For weeks, her family retreated to the sofa to eat.
The surface, the brush strokes, larger than life,
were reproduced down to the *craquelure*—
so real, yet a replica, yet very unlike the actual painting . . .

Which is what Walter Benjamin said in his essay
"The Work of Art in the Age of Mechanical Reproduction"—
how modern technology caused a "loss of aura,"
the special feeling that comes
when you view the work of art face to face.
The girl of *Girl with the Red Hat*, for example,
actually looking back at me looking at her,
our eyes locking, her face on a cocktail napkin
not a blotter for my lipstick.

In person, you can see for yourself the perfect
lines disappearing into a pinhole in the canvas—the vanishing point
around which were traced the angle
of trickling milk, the waterfall of sunbeams
streaming from a window, the exquisite icy pinprick
of light on a pearl.

from *Literary Imagination*

MARTHA SILANO

When I Learn Catastrophically

◇ ◇ ◇

is an anagram of *amyotrophic lateral sclerosis*.
When I learn I probably have a couple years,
maybe (catastrophically) less, crossword puzzles
begin to feel meaningless, though not the pair
of mergansers, not the red cardinal of my heart.
The sky does all sorts of marvelously uncatastrophic
things that winter I shimmy between science
& song, between widgeons & windows, weather
& its invitation to walk. Walking, which becomes
my *lose less*, my *less morsels*, my *lose smile*
while *more sore looms*. Sometimes I wander
for hours, my mile pace over half an hour,
everyone passing the lady at dusk talking
to herself about *looming rooms, soil lies, ire
& else*. Chuckling about my mileage gone down
the toilet, I plant the *rose* of before, the *oil* of after.
As each breath elevates to miracle, I become
both more & less of who I'd been, increasingly
less concerned about the dishes in the sink,
more worried about the words in my notebooks,
all those unfinished poems. I remember the fear
of getting lost if I left the main trail. I remember
molehills, actual molehills, piles of salty roe,
mountains of limes. Catastrophically, it's rare:
one in 500,000, but then I learned the odds
of being born: one in 42 billion, though not sure
how they calculate, or the chances of the cosmos
having just the right amount of force to not
break apart. *Less smiles. More lose. Miser miles.*

A sis & bro whom I'll leave like a sinking island,
Ferdinandea, that submerged volcano in Sicily,
though let's be real: I was more *pen mole* than *lava*,
more a looming annoyance than a bridge
to some continent. I'd wanted to be composted,
but it would cost 9K to convert me to dirt, so I opted
for whatever was easiest to carry across state lines,
some of me beside my mother & father, bits of me
on San Juan Island, at Jakle's Lagoon & Seward Park,
where I'd wandered like a *morose remorse*,
a *lore-less reel*, a *miser silo*, a doddering crow.

from *The Missouri Review*

Trio

◇ ◇ ◇

a. Driving Home from the Night Shift, Our Mother Listens to Hank Williams' "Lost Highway"

She cracks the window,
letting the cold air

    slap her awake. Cranking
    the radio, she sings

along as she leans
into the burn of Tiger

    Balm, her shift,
    like her body, a sharpening

of drill bits, the break
room doors. Soon,

    she'll enter the house
    before anyone is awake.

This is *her* time
when everything is still,

    when she could be
    anything—a thief,

a mouse. Alone,
she'll wipe coffee rings

       from counters, scrub
       sinks, floors. Love,

she'd tell you, is work, and work
is what remains

       when she leans into
       a sleep she can

almost taste, when
our father like the dawn

       rises to slip
       his arm around her waist.

b. My First Boyfriend and I Slow Dance to Jeff Buckley's Cover of Hank Williams' "Lost Highway"

This new voice is the old
voice of wanting

       what you already have.
       It marks me like

pressed hands in wet
cement, leaves me

       warm against a boy
       in a dorm room

damp with the musk
of hair gel,

       drugstore rubbers
       and knock-off Calvin Klein.

This is not romance.
This is not a story

        of easy need, though
        there's cheap beer

on the dresser,
rumpled white sheets

        on his unmade bed.
        Anything could happen—

his mother could call,
his roommate

        could walk in the door, or
        we could flinch,

dropping down as we inch
into each other, the track

        on repeat: *Now, boys, don't*
        start your ramblin' round . . .

Encore: Months Before His Overdose, Hank Williams Sings "Cold, Cold Heart" in 1952 on The Grand Ole Opry—YouTube, 2021

Here, as if brought to
life, the echo of some

        lost world: this skinny
        lightning-voiced angel

with his white cowboy
hat askew. Like death,

        the internet, I've read,
        is a ghostly well,

ever-expanding grave-
yard of last breaths.

> Is this, at last, what
> we're meant to become—

Hank's blazing eyes,
soulful black windows?

> He sings and sings,
> Byzantium's golden bird.

Or is this Christ's after-
life, gates ajar? Now,

> colorless, Hank strums
> his phantom guitar.

He stares. He blinks
and grins. He feels no pain.

> Strange beauty in the lie,
> this screen between

what's twice alive but
dead, what never ends.

> When he stops, I click
> back: he sings again.

from *The Georgia Review*

MOSAB ABU TOHA

Two Watches

◇ ◇ ◇

He's wearing two watches,
one set to the local time in New York,
the other to Gaza.

In a café with friends,
waiting for his tea at the round green table,
whenever his eyes fall
on the Gaza dial, he remembers the kids
of his neighborhood running in the alleys,
girls playing hopscotch, boys playing soccer.

At night, when the light in the Gaza watch doesn't work,
he knows electricity is off in his neighborhood.
If the metal case grows warm,
he knows bombs have started to fall.

If the watch doesn't move, he knows
a relative, a neighbor, a friend, has died.
When that happens, the watch won't work again
until the body is buried.

But what if there is no body anymore?

He is happy to have time, a watch that works.
He is happy to have time.

from *Ploughshares*

TONY TOWLE

Birthdays

◊ ◊ ◊

I wonder if Fernando Pessoa,
whose interest in astrology was intense,
when he wrote to William Butler Yeats
—whose interest matched his own—for advice
on establishing a national poetry for Portugal,
knew that they had the same birthday
and if he had known, would that
have persuaded him to actually send the letter
or could that have been why he *didn't* send it?
Forty-odd Junes ago I wondered about other things,
walking down West 18th Street, about to pass
the Chelsea post office, through whose door
directly in front of me, stepped John Ashbery.
After a mutual startled instant, he inquired mildly
in his celebrated nasal intonation: "What
are you doing on my *turf*?"—a reasonable question
since he knew I lived many blocks to the south.
Embarrassed, I answered, "You may not believe this,
but I'm going to see an astrologer" (a visit that Jean,
my girlfriend, had arranged as a birthday present).
Instead of acerbic admonishment on the imbecility
or worse of astrology, he asked: "It wouldn't
be Eleanor *Bach*, would it?" Stunned, I replied: "Yes,
as a matter of fact it would." While I settled into
relief, John informed me: "She does a lot of poets,"
and he mentioned several who were well-known
(though not personally by me), and then of course
he himself; and John related how she really impressed him
by persisting in a concern that there was something

off in his chart, something that didn't add up. Finally
he revealed a personal fact that had been withheld
and she said, "Oh, yes, it all makes sense now; why
didn't you tell me before?!" So I had been assured
by an esteemed literary figure that my personal incarnation
of the stellar and planetary intricacies would be rendered
with astute professional insight. Confidentially, though—
and I never told John—I thought that Ms. Bach
seemed too much concerned with my "rising" sign
to the neglect of my "sun" sign next door, regarding which,
and doubtless by the merest wisps of coincident genetic
and sociological meanders of fate, I am a first-class example.

from *Julebord* and *The Best American Poetry Blog*

CINDY TRAN

Blank Verse

◇ ◇ ◇

Lacking structure, I will say what I need
To say. My family fell apart for no good reason.
And for no bad reasons. It was the speed
Of being poor, genes turning off, a fire turning

On droughts, memories folding and unfolding
Across generations, like mountain ranges
Pushing up from the torn earth, molding
Distance by land and by air. What changes

The voice of a father from a father
To a stranger? It is the one question
I've been trying to answer for half my life.
I thought it was the '90s recession

Or my brother's private college tuition,
Or his mother's funeral in Vietnam
He couldn't afford to attend. Magician
Of History, tell me, was it the firebomb

Thrown onto the street of his old neighborhood?
God of Missing Stories, was it the lost
Meals and angry sisters of his childhood?
Universe of Eared Stars, whisper the cost

Of my father's own mother beating him
To teach him how to be a man. Someone
Once told me I looked like his mother: trim,
With a round face, big eyes and hair undone.

We've never met or spoken, but I imagine
We've met in my father's mind, tracing
His confusion and sadness. What would happen
Without this estrangement? We'd be facing

The other, from a different kind of distance.
I imagine he would buy me a balut
Because I loved it, had no resistance
When I was four years old, before I knew

What it was: a boiled embryo chicken.
Then he might disappear in the backyard
Smoking cigarettes and, to the trees, disclose
How much he didn't want to be a father.

The persimmons never judged him. But I did.
I was used to touching closed doors and hiding
In my home. Both of my parents prohibited
My sister and me from having friends, deciding

They were worth nothing and a waste of time,
Or else a danger to our family.
They thought they would be framed for a fake crime
And be sent all the way back across the sea

To live with war. The war never left them.
Years ago, I drove up the 405
Amid a wildfire that looked like the sum
Of all nine circles of Dante's hell alive,

Vanishing the entire sky. Feather ashes
Drifted down on my windshield like black snow.
As I drove through the fire, I saw flashes
Of my father as a boy, watching the glow

Of his street in flames. That fire never left me.
When I was fourteen, my boyfriend sent an email
To break up with me. I wish he could see
That when he appeared and told a tall tale

To my father   about how I'd stolen
His bike,   my father would believe him more
Because they're both   boys. That night, my father
Rammed his shoulder   into my bedroom door,

Broke it,   and said he disowned me forever.
Then he stopped talking to me   for four years.
It broke me. A father   who makes a sudden sever
Must be the unfolding   of random gears.

No amount of reason stops   the wondering.
Did he see   me grow up? Did he see me
Searching for him? Did he hear   the thundering
Of dusty years that would make us   both plea

With the air? Who steered him   to be a man
Of silence? Who abandoned us   to wars?
This morning,   I sat next to my dustpan
And listened   to all the cleanly closed doors

Between us. I no longer need   a father.
And tonight, I stand   beneath a starcliff—
Spirit of Small Chances,   help me remember
Just one good thing   I once loved about him.

from *The Southern Review*

Never Argue with the Movies

◊ ◊ ◊

1

In *To the Last Man*, a 1933 Western
about feuding families, Randolph Scott
is trying to get on with Esther Ralston
(unschooled and pretty wild). She
"ain't used to being polite at." He notices
that she's not wearing shoes. "It must
be sort of hard going barefoot through
these mountains." She takes offense:
"It's none of your business that I ain't
got shoes and stockin's." "I didn't mean
anything that way. They write poems
about barefoot girls like you." "What's
a poem?" she asks belligerently. "Oh,
a lot of words put together. They don't
mean anything, but they sound pretty good."

2

In *The Lives of a Bengal Lancer*, a 1935
adventure film, Gary Cooper and Franchot
Tone have both been tortured (bamboo
shoots under fingernails) and imprisoned
in a cell. Neither of them cracked under
pressure; they're true heroes. Shortly before
the explosive finale, Tone quotes Lewis Carroll:
" 'The time has come,' the Walrus said, /
'To talk of many things: / Of shoes—and ships—
and sealing-wax— / Of cabbages—and kings—' "
"Oh, shut up!" barks Coop. "You don't like
poetry?" "How should I know, I never read any."

3

In *Evelyn Prentice*, a 1934 crime drama, Myrna Loy receives a book in the mail from a supposed admirer (actually a gigolo) she met at a nightclub. "*Bonjour*," says her friend Una Merkel when she joins her for breakfast. (Her French is a charming affectation.) "Don't tell me you go in for early morning reading. What's the book?" "It's called *Sonnets to the Sun*," replies Loy. "What to the which?" "*Sonnets to the Sun*. Pretty, isn't it? It's a book of poems." "Poems? In the morning? Darling, it's your liver." Loy reads her the letter that came with it. "Oh, the good-looking thrill with broad shoulders," coos Merkel, when she realizes who it's from. "Go on." "*I'm taking the liberty of sending you, along with this letter, a book of my poems.*" "A poet," sighs Merkel, "It's an awful waste of broad shoulders." "Ever hear of him?" "*Je n'ai pas.*" "Neither have I. Coffee?"

from *R&R*

BERNARD WELT

The Story So Far

◊ ◊ ◊

It was a hard birth, in an upper berth, to a woman named Bertha
and a man named Bert. Sad that they were destined never to meet.
I was adopted by a truly lovely couple, of a variety of extractions.
Their roots were in olde England and New South Wales, and old
southern Wales where stalwart farriers dug the obdurate coal
out of the deep unyielding earth, where they put their shoulder
to the wheel and their feet on the ground, their knees up
and their hands to themselves; and colorful Bessarabia
and drab Slovenia and Hungary and Brittany and Brindaban
and Bhutan and Cathay and Mandalay and Hunan and Sichuan
and Iowa and Ohio and Idaho and the Midwest, the Middle East
and Middle Earth, and the hinterlands of the lowlands of the badlands
of the Southland. And that is why, they said, they had the gift of gab
and the wisdom of the ages and the patience of a saint and a nose
for news and the good sense they were born with and hearts
as big as all outdoors and eyes bigger than their stomachs and names
to conjure with and a busman's holiday and a cobbler's eyetooth
and a costermonger's chance. As it happened, the couple who adopted me
were also my biological parents, so it was almost as if it were fated.
My progenitors were very rich and very poor, by turns and finally
at the same time. I acquired skills, incredible and of no use.
I kept them to myself. I profited by the labor of my hands
and the skin of my teeth. I got a job, and then the job got me.
I was a gofer. I wondered what to go for. You probably know
what I went for. I gave them what for. I considered the consequences.

I sang like an angel. I danced like the wind. I talked too much.
I talked too much. I talked too much. I talked too much.

I reside in a modest house known locally as "The Estate" with my husband, my wife, my girlfriend, my boyfriend, my girlfriend's boyfriend, my boyfriend's girlfriend, my girlfriend's boyfriend's boyfriend, two sons, one daughter, one stepdaughter, two stepsons, a son-in-law, an outlaw son, a grandson, a great-grandson, a not-so-hot grandson, a layabout, a scoundrel, a wastrel, a mongrel, a rat, a bat, a cat, a dog, a hog, and a frog named Gog and Magog, with an azalea, a hydrangea, a camellia, and a bougainvillea, in a pergola festooned with wisteria, and in the front yard a single petunia, a begonia, forget-me-nots and love-lies-bleeding. I got the pergola because I'm a faygeleh.

My existence was aimless. My life had no direction. I lost my moral compass. I wandered lonely as a cloud. I came from outer space. I ate the air before me. The stars were my destination. I had reached the last outpost. My time had come. I studied history. I made history. I was history. I gave up the ghost. I cashed in my chips. I saw that all was vanity. I bought the farm. I wrote my memoirs:

I Didn't Do It! . . . Or Did I?
Present at My Autopsy
My Life as a Beard—No, I Mean the Kind on Your Face
How to Get Stains Out of Practically Everything . . . Except Your Heart
That Time I Was on TV
Hope for the Best and Spend Your Life Stewing in Disappointed Dreams
Egg Salad for Two
This Is Not Your Father's Egg Salad
I Never Promised You an Egg Salad
The Man from Hanukkah
You Can't Call It Brunch if You're Eating Alone
Nobody Knows the Minor Inconvenience I've Seen
Money Cheerfully Refunded Upon Request.

I can tell you, of my own experience: Life is too short and moves too fast. The days succeed the nights, but the nights outlast the days. With dawn comes a reckoning. Night falls like a drunk stumbling down stairs. Day breaks like a twig in a strong man's grip. Go out the door. Get out your handkerchiefs. Listen to the rhythm of the falling rain.

Listen again. Look at the sky. Look at the earth. Look
where you're going. Look out for me. Stay out of my way.
Write when you find work. Give me your blessing before you go.
Be mine. Be there for me. Be yourself. Be someone else.
I'll catch you round the campus. I'll see you in my dreams.
I'll be wherever you are. Lately some of my friends have been insisting
that I'm actually dead, and have been for some time, but I think
that's just because I can be pretty hard to get in touch with.
Where I come from—well, people just don't come from there.

                from *Gargoyle*

LESLEY WHEELER

Sex Talk

◇ ◇ ◇

After a fight, men want to have sex, but I don't, my mother said.
She glanced at undergraduate me from the driver's seat as if a membrane

had been breached and asked, Do you?

                                          I wanted to change the subject.
We were returning from the mall through the stony suburb

where the model lived, the one who said, *Nothing comes between me
and my Calvins,* where the fire department floods the common

every winter for skating, creating warty ice ungroomed by Zambonis,
grass snagged in its skin like ingrown hairs. My mother kept looking

at me, her eye a sideways question mark, tricky liquid liner painted
along the lid, pupil unrelenting.

                          Everyone in the family except

my mother owned their own lockable room. She had to read her Harlequins
out in the open like a gazelle. We stalked through, asking and asking:

where is the, why can't I, help me. Nightly her shirtless husband
arrived with a pump-jar of Jergens demanding she moisturize his back,

scaly from chlorine, but I knew—spy crouching on the stairs,
fingertips brushing wallpaper embossed with creamy trees,

its surface all bubbles and seams—what he was after.

Once at a Modernism conference a guy chased me around the canapés

while lecturing me on Marianne Moore's asexuality.
I knew my mother didn't like sex, but I never asked

was it generally or just sex with my father. Nothing
gets between me and my shame.

I don't know what Moore wanted,
just that she wrote cryptic poems under her mother's surveillance.

Heterosexual marriage: she, too, disliked it. She was nearly sixty
when her mother died.

                        Now I know death's intimacy.

How honesty frightens me. My mother is everywhere:
cells lodged in my body, invisible flakes of skin on sweaters,

a baggie of ashes on the bookshelf.

                              Not after a fight.
Until adrenaline burns off, I'm hot the wrong way. Clenched.

I hope she knew what an orgasm feels like. (During my first,
a rainbow tree grew between me and my eyelids, privately.)

She said to us, over her book, *No, I don't want
to hug you goodnight.*

                    from *The Gettysburg Review* and *Poetry Daily*

GEOFFREY YOUNG

The How and When of It

◊   ◊   ◊

We were not alone in San Diego in the fifties. Bobby Smith's father
George was a beer drunk who sold used cars. Dickie's father Leon,
A butcher, was too. Dickie and fam lived across the street with Grandpa
Duffield who wore uniform grey clothes, rolled his own, sat in a haze
Of smoke all day and made the memorably horrible sounds of spitting

Into a spittoon. We didn't yet have a TV, and theirs was always on.
Boxing was big (we watched Sugar Ray Robinson beat Bobo Olson).
We took in the spectacle of wrestling (Gorgeous George preening),
And Roller Derby (tough women elbowing each other in the ribs
As they pumped and rolled). There were other fathers, as well,

Who weren't lushes, I'm sure, but they remained out of sight.
Mike's father, Mr Schmidt, worked for Budweiser. Mike and I
Would come home from school and spin 45s, listening to "Buick 59"
By The Medallions & Little Richard's "Rip It Up" and "Ready Teddy,"
Among the many. "Stranded in the Jungle"? One day Mike's mother

Said she was sorry to read in the papers that my parents had divorced.
I said, "What?" News to me, at age twelve. The Schmidts had just been
Visited by their old friend Don Larsen, Yankee World Series hero
Who'd pitched a perfect game. When I got home I walked into the kitchen
And asked about what I'd just heard. Mom said, "Oh yes, I was going

To tell you boys. I don't believe in divorce but your father insisted."

from *Live Mag!* and the Chaudiere Books blog

KEVIN YOUNG

Snapdragon

◊ ◊ ◊

Of late the dead
    have quit
their midnight

visits. They ask
    to swing by
sometime, without

ringing first—
    Thank you, no.
Think I'll stay here,

friends, in sunlight
    at the start
of summer, the snapdragons

& daylilies bright
    my son plucks.

Down the road
    the dandelions bloom
in a garden of stone.

A garland of souls.

Like the vines
    I'll climb—
like children who join

their limbs to the silver
maple's, waving
to all who pass on by.

from *The American Poetry Review*

CONTRIBUTORS' NOTES AND COMMENTS

GBENGA ADESINA was born in Akure, Nigeria, in 1989 and was raised there and in Lagos. He was a Goldwater Poetry Fellow at New York University, where he received his MFA in poetry and was mentored by Yusef Komunyakaa. At Colgate University, as the 2019–2020 Olive B. O'Connor Poetry Fellow, he taught a poetry class called Song of the Human. He received a PhD in English from Florida State. *Death Does Not End at the Sea*, his first book of poems, won the 2024 Prairie Schooner Book Prize and was published in fall 2025 by the University of Nebraska Press.

Of "The People's History of 1998," Adesina writes: "I have always believed poetry is the eloquence of what is veiled by history. I'm always thinking about the poetry of history, not history as historians define it (great figures and achievements, wars, presidents, treaties, great speeches), but the history of feeling, the history of desire, the history of grief, the history of ordinary dailiness, the history of the disregarded, the history of those trapped in the cruelty of power. The summer I wrote the poem, I was homesick and thinking about my parents and siblings and childhood a lot, the milieu, the cultural, political, and emotional atmosphere of the world in which I grew up in Akure, a quiet town southwest of Nigeria. We lived in a small corner of the globe, but we were always aware of the world. And we knew by some inexplicable instinct that the world was our future destination. News of that destination filtered through to us through movies, sports, political news, and literature. When I think of 1998, I think of France winning the World Cup in a final match against Brazil (3–0) with two spectacular headers by the enigmatic, not-yet-bald Zinedine Zidane. We all rushed out into the backyard singing 'Un, deux, trois! Ale, Ale, Ale!' and later in the day tried to replicate some of his skillful moves on a small patch where we played soccer. When I think of 1998, I think of the day the news came to us that the dark-goggled dictator (General

Sani Abacha) who tyrannized our lives, but was mostly myth, legend, and dark rumors to my childhood ears, died.

"A contagion of joy spread through all the homes and neighborhood. Adults, including my parents, rushed out to the streets, dancing, hugging each other, singing, shedding ecstatic tears. It was as if all the houses were without walls and there were no barriers between us, and we were all children of the same history, yet in my family we had our private griefs. It's something I'm still working on, how to let poetry tell a history that belongs to all of us yet is braided with each family's solitude, a history of the chorus that is also a history of private griefs and desire."

Hussain Ahmed was born in Nigeria in 1991. He is the author of *Soliloquy with the Ghosts in Nile* (Black Ocean, 2022) and *Blue Exodus* (Orison Books, 2024). He holds an MFA from the University of Mississippi and is completing a doctorate at the University of Cincinnati.

Of "Incantation for a Lake," Ahmed writes: "The event that led to this poem remains vivid in my mind. I wore an embroidered yellow caftan, one of the many that my father gave me before I left Nigeria. It was the week after the Covid-19 vaccinations started rolling out, and the idea of social distancing was still new. I had arrived at Houston's airport on Christmas Eve of 2019 and later found my way to Mississippi, where I was to resume my MFA. A few months after my arrival, the outbreak was announced, and even though the lockdown reminded me of the Sufi tradition of Khalwa, I was scared. In the despair of those early pandemic days, I was heartbroken with the possibility of dying in America, where I had come to dream. After the restrictions were lowered, we started gathering in the Oxford mosque, and in that first day, another Nigerian friend who drives me to pray told me he needed to get a spare part for his Toyota and asked that I accompany him to a mechanic shop somewhere out of town, where he was told he'd get cheap car parts. I followed him and we were faced with the shop owner, who made jokes about guns and the places around Africa where he had served, places he thought I would know, when I told him I was from Nigeria. This poem is my thanksgiving note for surviving that one day in the pandemic."

Born in Colombo, Ceylon, in 1960, Indran Amirthanayagam is a poet, editor, publisher, translator, YouTube host, and diplomat. For thirty years he worked for his adoptive country, the United States, on diplomatic assignments in Africa, Asia, Europe, and North and South America. Amirthanayagam writes in English, Spanish, French, Portuguese, and Haitian Creole; in 2020, he published three poetry collections written in three different languages. He edits the *Beltway Poetry Quarterly* and Beltway Editions, blogs at indranamirthanayagam.blogspot.com, and writes a weekly poem for *Haiti en Marche* and *El Acento*.

Amirthanayagam notes: "I wrote 'At the Gate' during the last year of caring for my late mother, who suffered from gradual memory loss and the increasing inability to move. I cared for her with Marianne, my Haitian friend and staff. I remember my mother trying to get up in bed one day and failing, raising her hands and shrugging: *I cannot. You can take me to a home now*.

"My mother taught me courage and patience. She prayed and kept counsel with God and her memories, her desires, and her dreams, some achieved and some unmet. She wanted to return to her home in Ceylon. She wanted to go to university. She was the top of her class in secondary school, but as the campus where she could study English literature was several hours away from home, at Peradeniya, in the Hill Country, her father did not approve. She married instead and devoted her learning to raising five children, to teaching us to be proud of our roots and the new lands where we remade our lives, in London, Honolulu, Rockville.

"My mother taught me to read. Caring for her taught me more deeply to love. That love flows through this poem. I wrote a villanelle for her as Dylan Thomas wrote one for his father. The pattern gives the lines some matter. They can be remembered. I remain essentially a poet in free verse, but I have written many free sonnets and four-beat blues poems. And there is hardly a poem I write these days that does not look ordered and neat on the page."

MARGARET ATWOOD was born in Ottawa, Ontario, in 1939. *Paper Boat: New and Selected Poems, 1961–2023* was published in 2024. Her novels include *Cat's Eye*, *The Robber Bride*, *Alias Grace*, *The Blind Assassin*, and the *Madd Addam* trilogy. Her 1985 classic, *The Handmaid's Tale*, was followed in 2019 by a sequel, *The Testaments*, which was a global number one bestseller and won the Booker Prize. In 2020 she published *Dearly*, her first collection of poetry in a decade, followed in 2022 with

Burning Questions, a selection of essays from 2004 to 2021. In 2019 she was made a member of the Order of the Companions of Honour for services to literature. She has also worked as a cartoonist, illustrator, librettist, playwright, and puppeteer. She lives in Toronto, Canada.

CATHERINE BARNETT is the author of four poetry collections: *Solutions for the Problem of Bodies in Space* (Graywolf Press, 2024), *Human Hours* (Graywolf, 2018), *The Game of Boxes* (Graywolf, 2012), and *Into Perfect Spheres Such Holes Are Pierced* (Alice James Books, 2004). A Guggenheim and Civitella Ranieri Fellow, she has received *The Believer* Book Award, a James Laughlin Award from the Academy of American Poets, a Whiting Award, and a 2022 Arts and Letters Award in Literature. She teaches in the NYU creative writing program and works as an independent editor.

Of "Nicholson Baker and I," Barnett writes: "When I was a young writer, I came across Nicholson Baker's *U and I: A True Story*, which taught me a lot—in the most pleasurable way—about literary obsession and imaginary friendship. This poem is my side of an imaginary friendship. *A Box of Matches* is the text mentioned at the end of the poem, a book that inspires my practice of writing every day, trying to notice whatever there is to notice (in both the interior and exterior worlds, though of course the demarcation between these worlds is blurry, permeable). Like the narrator of that novel, who I imagine is a character very close to Baker himself, I too carry spiders out of my home in a drinking glass, but I don't sing 'Eight Days a Week' while showering."

DAVID BEAUDOUIN, native to Baltimore, Maryland, founded Tropos Press (1976–2001), one of the region's earliest and most respected alternative literary presses, as well as *THE PEARL* (1980–2001), a Baltimore journal of the literary and "spontaneous" arts. He served for more than a decade as a literary panelist for the Mayor's Committee on Arts and Culture and was instrumental in the creation of the Artscape Literary Arts Award. David has collaborated with the visual artists Julia Kim Smith and Thea Osato on multimedia projects, and has coproduced two documentary shorts, *Fluid Movement* and *One Nice Thing*. A new collection, *On Down the Line* (UnCollected Press), was published in 2025.

Of "Annunciation," Beaudouin writes: "From O'Hara to Olson, many poets have set their sense of personal place as the axis for their work. My city of Baltimore has infused much of the context of my poems over the years, although I avoided addressing my point on that map until I knew how to say what I already felt. Ted Berrigan's poem 'Whitman in Black' provided the key. Put it on the cuff, Ted."

DONALD BERGER is the author of six books of poetry: *The Rose of Maine* (SurVision Books, 2024), *Pizza Necklace* (Foundlings Press, 2023), *The Long Time*, a bilingual edition in English and German (Wallstein Publishers, Göttingen, Germany, 2014), *Or Purchase a Star* (Jiddizig Books, 2008), *Quality Hill* (Lost Roads Publishers, 1993), and *The Cream-Filled Muse* (Fledermaus Press, 1988). He has received a Fulbright Fellowship and the James Tate International Poetry Prize. He teaches in the University Writing Program at Johns Hopkins University.

Of "Uncle Sadness," Berger writes: "This poem is a narrative-epistle made up mainly of images I gathered while traveling in Hong Kong, and the speaker addresses his listener from this city. From a notebook or two written around the time of the trip, I chose phrases that I found most striking and went from there. You'll notice that there's a bit of jumping around, which I hope the reader will accept and even enjoy. I assembled the stanzas in a pattern of thought, feeling, and observation that I imagine someone might actually experience, moving back and forth between the speaker's concrete surroundings and his internal world."

CAMILLE CARTER was born in Kansas in 1993. She lives and teaches in New York, where she is pursuing her PhD in comparative literature.

Of "Thoughts about Inheritance," Carter writes: "This poem plays with the idea of wealth as envisioned through paucity, an exploration of thinking through the complicated implications of what we are and are not bequeathed, what we are willed by the world, by others living and dead—and what we will in turn. In writing this poem, I was thinking about the coin as an ideogram of power, as a paradoxical value-marker, as ritual material of human wish-making, and as the ubiquitous object that litters the ground; this became, for me, a natural means to consider the (meta)physical implications of pockets, their depth, the prospect or reality of their emptiness, the transactional nature of human relations, and, of course, the costliness of dreams."

GRACE CAVALIERI was Maryland's tenth Poet Laureate, from 2018 to 2024. Her recent poetry books are *Fables from Italy and Beyond* (Bordighera Press, 2025), *I Haiku Too* (Bunny and Crocodile Press, 2024), *Owning the Not So Distant World* (Blue Light Press, 2024), and *The Long Game: New & Selected Poems* (The Word Works, 2023). Cavalieri founded and still produces *The Poet and the Poem* for public radio, now from the Library of Congress, celebrating forty-eight years on air. She has written twenty-five plays produced on American stages; the most recent, *Quilting the Sun*, is about ex-slave quiltmaker Harriet Powers. The last twenty-five years of Cavalieri's podcasts have been sent to the moon from NASA on Lunar Codex, landing in the Ocean of Storms.

Cavalieri writes: "It is true that 'White Suit' is autobiographical and shamelessly accurate in time, place, and happenstance. Yet it is important to note, after that disastrous reunion, the subjects of the poem enjoyed sixty married years with four children, four grandchildren, and a great-grandson." Grace Cavalieri's late husband was Kenneth Flynn, renowned metal sculptor and former naval aviator.

CHRISTOPHER CHAMBERS was born in Wisconsin in 1960 and has since lived in North Carolina, Michigan, Minnesota, Florida, Alabama, Texas, and Louisiana. He is the author of three books—*Kind of Blue* (Cornerstone Press, 2022), *Inter/views* (Calumet Editions, 2021), and *Delta 88* (Split Oak Press, 2013)—and coeditor of the anthology *Ice Fishing for Alligators* (Calumet, 2021).

Chambers writes: "What can I say about 'What About This,' except that it was written in New Orleans, on the occasion of a secondhand copy of Frank Stanford's handsome book, *What About This*, appearing in my mailbox. As I write this today, that book, without which I would not have written 'What About This,' sits on my desk more or less as described. I don't recall much about the poem's origins or evolution, but I can say that in addition to Stanford's book, it is beholden to the work of C. D. Wright, Everette Maddox, Ralph Adamo, Lucinda Williams, and Miller Williams. And now that I think of it, there's an Amazon review of Thomas Bernhard's collection *Prose*, posted by one W. Wilson (check it out—the book and the review!), which may also have had something to do with the way 'What About This' ultimately spun out onto the page. How about that?"

Born in 1989 in Albany, New York, DOROTHY CHAN is the author of five poetry collections: *Return of the Chinese Femme* (Deep Vellum Publishing, 2024), *BABE* (Diode Editions, 2021), *Revenge of the Asian Woman* (Diode, 2019), *Attack of the Fifty-Foot Centerfold* (Spork Press, 2018), and the chapbook *Chinatown Sonnets* (New Delta Review, 2017). They are an associate professor of English at the University of Wisconsin–Eau Claire and cofounder of *Honey Literary*.

Of "Triple Sonnet for Nomi Malone," Chan writes: "I was once a lonely queer kid who spent the weekends watching movies and runway shows on TV, creating my own worlds. Though Turner Classic Movies was usually my channel of choice, I remember stumbling upon (the TV-appropriate version of) *Showgirls* and becoming transfixed by the scene where Nomi is sitting atop the iconic Flamingo Hotel, eating a burger and fries. At least, that's how I remember it."

HEATHER CHRISTLE was born in Wolfeboro, New Hampshire, in 1980. She is the author of five poetry collections, most recently *Paper Crown* (Wesleyan University Press, 2025). She also writes prose, including *In the Rhododendrons: A Memoir with Appearances by Virginia Woolf* (Algonquin Books, 2025). She teaches creative writing at Emory University.

Christle writes: "'Aubade' is one of many poems—a whole book, in fact!—whose lines can each stand as its own syntactic unit. I like to think of the lines as rungs on an erratic ladder one must climb down to read. Or to write. I never know how near or far down I am going to have to dangle my foot to catch the next rung, but so far my steps continue to (eventually) return me to a place where I can hop off and go do something else."

LOR CLINCY was born in Kissimmee, Florida, when her parents were on vacation in 1996. She is a Chicago resident, educator, poet, and entrepreneur. She is a cofounder and nonfiction editor of *Unwoven Literary & Arts Magazine*, a Chicago-based publication and collective of writers.

Clincy writes: "'Wishes for Black Women' was born out of necessity. I thought deeply about everything I wished for, and while power and influence could have easily been number one on my list, Black women need so much more. Respite, peace, and rest are sometimes far out of reach for us. We are a culture of matriarchy and tremendous willpower. Our journeys require revisioning and revival of a long-standing experience with trauma and institutional distraught that follows us every day of our lives. In this piece, I explore the possibilities of a world in which we are not burdened by who, *what* we are."

ANDREA COHEN was born in Atlanta, Georgia, in 1961. She is the author of eight poetry collections, including, most recently, *The Sorrow Apartments* (Four Way Books, 2024), *Everything* (Four Way, 2021), and *Nightshade* (Four Way, 2019). The recipient of a Guggenheim Fellowship and several fellowships at MacDowell, she directs the Blacksmith House Poetry Series in Cambridge, Massachusetts, and teaches at Boston University.

Of "Fable," Cohen writes: "Some time ago I went back to my old high school in Atlanta and met with some students. One of them asked, 'Why do you have so many poems that reference the Bible?' Somehow, until he'd asked that, I hadn't quite realized how those stories—those really good stories I was brought up on—were part of me, and thus kept resurfacing. The same is true for fables. I read them as a child, had them read to me, and they're in me—as is this propensity to interrogate/muse on the old myths and see how I might bang on them and reshape them a little."

BILLY COLLINS was born in the French Hospital in New York City in 1941. He graduated from the College of the Holy Cross and received his PhD from the University of California, Riverside. His books of poetry include *Water, Water* (Random House, 2024), *Musical Tables* (Random House, 2022), *Aimless Love: New and Selected Poems* (Random House, 2013), a collection of haiku titled *She Was Just Seventeen* (Modern Haiku Press, 2006), *The Trouble with Poetry and Other Poems* (Random House, 2005), *Picnic, Lightning* (University of Pittsburgh Press, 1998), *The Art of Drowning* (Pittsburgh, 1995), and *Questions About Angels* (William Morrow, 1991), which was selected for the National Poetry Series by Edward Hirsch and reprinted by the University of Pittsburgh Press in 1999. A former Distinguished Professor of English at Lehman College (City University of New York), he is a frequent contributor to and former guest editor of *The Best American Poetry* series. He was appointed United States Poet Laureate (2001–2003), served as New York State Poet (2004–2006), and was recently inducted into the American Academy of Arts and Letters.

Of "Thought a Rarity on Paper," Collins writes: "This is a poem in the form of a thank-you note, or a thank-you note in the form of a poem. The currents running beneath are poetry and friendship—specifically, my long friendship with Jesuit college classmate Tom Wallace, and later with Chris Calhoun, the pal who gave me the book of Jack Spicer's poems as a present. The feel of the book in my hands brought me back to my days with Tom in North Beach in the mid-sixties. Tom and I didn't know Spicer well, but he always recognized us, and we, 'the Jesuits,' even got a mention in his biography, *Poet Be Like God*. At the time, Tom and I were aspiring poets who felt a combination of idolatry and bitter jealousy toward the real ones, especially the older ones talking at the end of the bar while we were singing youthfully at the jukebox. To hide our literary seriousness, we modeled ourselves after that pair of louche wisecrackers in *Candy*, Tom Kat and Dick Smart. We would indulge in the music and drugs of the Haight when it came along, but we always felt more at home in North Beach with the grounded habits of literature and alcohol. Of course, we held publication in contempt.

"In the poem, the reverie ends with a sweep of mortality as Spicer dies, then Tom, leaving me here with Chris's present, a little green and gray book, which flies from my hands on the wings of loneliness and invention as the poem recedes into the background of an ever-changing sky."

KATIE CONDON was born in Milford, Connecticut, in 1990. Her first book, *Praying Naked*, won the Charles B. Wheeler poetry prize and was published by the Ohio State University Press in 2020. She received a 2025 National Endowment for the Arts Fellowship and was the 2023 Nadya Aisenberg Fellow at MacDowell. She holds an MFA in poetry from the University of Houston, and a PhD in English from the University of Tennessee. She teaches creative writing at Southern Methodist University, where she is an assistant professor of English.

Of "Book Blurb in the American Style," Condon writes: "I'm both wary of and delighted by the overly eager book blurb. On the one hand, it's impossible that each of this year's thirty-seven poetry collections whose blurbists claim they will be 'indelibly immortalized in the canon for all of time' actually will be, and isn't that a grotesquely unfair amount of pressure to put on artists to prove the claim true? On the other hand, I'm sympathetic to the fact that the overpromising book blurb is just a symptom of capitalism, and if we're forced to make and distribute art under this profit-motivated regime, why *not* have fun with it, why not make the blurb a piece of performance art in and of itself?

"Ten years ago in a Houston coffee shop, a friend and I were mulling over all of this capitalism and art stuff. Out of that puzzling we gave ourselves the prompt to concoct farcical jacket copy for ourselves, to use the conventions of America's consumerist enterprise to satirize it. 'Book Blurb in the American Style' was the result of that prompt, and I'm so happy that it's found homes in *Copper Nickel* and now here. The irony that, of all my poems, 'Book Blurb in the American Style' has landed in the best of the 'Best of' anthologies delights me to no end. I'm sincerely honored that this poem was selected, even if I'm also relieved that I won't be around to know whether people are still reading it in a hundred years."

Born in 1970 in Moncks Corner, South Carolina, MORRI CREECH is the author of five books of poetry, including *The Sleep of Reason* (Waywiser Press, 2013), *Blue Rooms* (Waywiser, 2018), and most recently *The Sentence* (LSU Press, 2023). A recipient of NEA and Ruth Lilly Fellowships, as well as grants from the Louisiana and North Carolina Arts Councils, he teaches at Queens University of Charlotte in North Carolina.

Creech writes: "I wrote 'A Letter from Rome' for my friend, the poet Joseph Harrison, who died of cancer in February of 2024; I finished the poem in the summer of 2023, a few months before his diagnosis. The piece attempts to express some of the anxieties Joe and I both felt about the festering political instabilities of the age."

PATRICIA DAVIS-MUFFETT was born in Willingboro, New Jersey, in 1970. She is the author of a chapbook, *Alchemy of Yeast and Tears* (Kelsay Books, 2023). She was the 2024 winner of the Erskine J. Poetry Prize from *Smartish Pace*, and Marge Piercy chose her poems several times for a placement in the Joe Gouveia Outermost Poetry Contest. She lives in Rockville, Maryland, with her husband and holds an MFA from the University of Minnesota.

Davis-Muffett writes: "'Climate Anxiety' came out of my long marriage to my amazing husband, Carroll Muffett, who has dedicated his life to fighting for climate justice. He has always been a visionary and has worked on climate change since the 1990s—when he sketched out worst-case scenarios we are now living through. Being his life partner means that I am the person who can most see the toll this work takes on him (and so many others engaged in this fight for the long haul), since he does not have the luxury of giving in to despair, even knowing what he knows. As he often says to me, 'The only hope lies in action.' This poem is the opening poem in my new manuscript, *Premature Elegy*, which mourns what has been and will be lost, while tracing the contours of a love that has grown over time, imagining a future without this partner. It is an elegy for the earth and an elegy for long love."

ARMEN DAVOUDIAN was born in 1990 in Isfahan, Iran, where he grew up before immigrating to the United States in 2008. He is the author of the poetry collection *The Palace of Forty Pillars* (Tin House Books, US, and Corsair, UK, 2024) and the translator, from Persian, of *Hopscotch* by Fatemeh Shams (Ugly Duckling Presse, 2024).

GREG DELANTY was born in Cork City, Ireland, in 1958. Delanty's latest collections are *The Professor of Forgetting* (2023) and *No More Time* (2020), both from LSU Press. He teaches at Saint Michael's College, Vermont, and has lived in Burlington since 1986. He has received a Guggenheim Fellowship, and in 2021 he was awarded the David Ferry and Ellen LaForge Poetry Prize. Recently one of his poems, "The Alien," appeared in Wes Anderson's movie *Asteroid City*. His website is gregdelanty.com.

Delanty writes: "I am grateful to the editor and poet Jana Prikryl at *The New York Review of Books* for first publishing 'To Our Indolent Cancer,' for a number of reasons. Outside of it being accepted, the poem was accepted less than two hours after I emailed a small selection of poems to her, and also Jana suggested changes that made the poem more successful. The poem is from a hybrid book of poems and prose I am still working on, *The Cancer Chorus*. Many of the poems written for it are in 'the royal *we*,' nosism pronoun poems. Almost all of the poems, including 'To Our Indolent Cancer,' of the projected book are also written in what 'we' are calling accordion sonnets, which sometimes compress to less than fourteen lines and sometimes they are much longer, one as long as forty-two lines, but with the same general rhyme scheme, though unlike 'To Our Indolent Cancer' many finish with a rhyming couplet. They are sonnets to and about my cancer and my corpus."

ABIGAIL DEMBO was born in Los Alamos, New Mexico, in 1981. She received her Bachelor of Arts in English from the University of California, Berkeley. She has lived most of her adult life in the Bay Area, but currently resides in Iowa City, where she is a student at the Iowa Writers' Workshop.

Dembo writes: "'The Travelers' began, I think, with my own sense of nostalgia. It seemed once the poem made a place to house this feeling, all sorts of memories, regrets, and desires began to accrue. The memory of waking to the sound of chickens in a neighbor's yard, of a woman playing piano in the living room, stories of my father's family history, of my mother's childhood, moments from my childhood books were drawn into the scene. Soon, I began to feel as though I was creating a place held in common, where even the simplest subtle longings might be acknowledged. The finches, for example, were borrowed from my mother's childhood, in which, at the age of seven, she was unable to save her birds from a house fire. All of this, staged within a somewhat ominous, bureaucratic, dusty world, suspiciously out of date."

JOSE HERNANDEZ DIAZ is a 2017 NEA Poetry Fellow from Los Angeles, California. He is the author of *Bad Mexican, Bad American* (Acre Books, 2024), *The Parachutist* (Sundress, 2025), and *Portrait of the Artist as a Brown Man* (Red Hen Press, 2025).

Diaz writes: "This prose poem was written after a similar experience in real life. I woke up to my Twitter account hacked. I was able to solve the problem after many of my Twitter followers reported the account hacked. I used the frustrating experience as inspiration and went with the Kafkaesque vibe to help turn the experience into an absurdist prose poem where the internet or AI essentially takes over. I initially had the title 'My Kafka Diary,' and the sharp editor at *The Southern Review* suggested 'My Kafka Prose Poem.'"

TISHANI DOSHI was born in Madras, India, in 1975. She is a poet, novelist, and dancer whose work centers on the body as a vehicle to explore gender, sexuality, and power. Her most recent books are a collection of poems, *A God at the Door* (Copper Canyon Press, 2021), and a novel, *Small Days and Nights* (W. W. Norton, 2020). She is a fellow of the British Royal Society of Literature and a visiting associate professor at New York University, Abu Dhabi.

Of "Egrets, While War," Doshi writes: "Something about the circularity of loss and survival and observing the egrets in my garden and their funny dance. How we are connected, have always been connected, have feared, continue to fear, long for wholeness, but are left with fragments. I think that's what I was trying to say with the poem."

DENISE DUHAMEL was born in Providence, Rhode Island, in 1961. Her most recent books of poetry include *Pink Lady* (University of Pittsburgh Press, 2025), *Second Story* (Pittsburgh, 2021), *Scald* (Pittsburgh, 2017), and *Blowout* (Pittsburgh, 2013). *In Which* (Pittsburgh, 2024) won the Rattle Chapbook Prize. She and the late Maureen Seaton coauthored five collections, the most recent of which are *Tilt* (Bridwell Press, 2025) and *CAPRICE: Collaborations—Collected, Uncollected, and New* (Sibling Rivalry Press, 2015). Duhamel's book of lyric essays with Julie Marie Wade is *The Unrhymables: Collaborations in Prose* (Noctuary Press, 2019). A recipient of an NEA grant and Guggenheim Fellowship, Duhamel is a distinguished university professor at Florida International University in Miami. She was the guest editor for *The Best American Poetry 2013*.

Duhamel writes: "This poem comes from a series of 'in which' poems that first started as alternative realities—poems in which I never became a poet, poems in which I am a cartoon or a corpse. 'Poem in Which This Fathead "Fat Ass" Admits It' sprang into a different territory altogether, poems that engage with sentiments I'd rather not admit. This is a mea culpa poem. Think William Carlos Williams—that is, if he were truly sorry about eating those plums."

ELAINE EQUI was born in Oak Park, Illinois, in 1953. She is the author of ten collections of poetry, including *Voice-Over* (Coffee House Press, 1998), which was chosen by Thom Gunn for the San Francisco State Poetry Center Book Award; *Ripple Effect: New & Selected Poems* (Coffee

House, 2007); and, most recently, *Out of the Blank* (Coffee House, 2025). She was guest editor of *The Best American Poetry 2023*. In 2024, she received a Guggenheim Fellowship.

Of "Lorca's Guitar," Equi writes: "Many years ago, I saw his guitar in a wonderful exhibit at the New York Public Library. The show, called 'Back Tomorrow: Federico García Lorca / Poet in New York,' featured letters, photos, drawings, and drafts of poems all from the year (1929–1930) when Lorca, then enrolled as a student at Columbia University, was writing what would become one of his darkest and most powerful collections, *Poet in New York*. There was a wealth of fascinating documents to explore, but what I spent the most time contemplating was a personal artifact—Lorca's actual guitar. I was transfixed. I stood before it as if at a shrine. I listened intently as if it were a radio or a jukebox. The guitar was such an intimate partner and part of Lorca's writing process; music—an animating connective tissue in his work. He collected Andalusian folk songs; he reimagined gypsy ballads; he crafted his aesthetic notion of duende inspired in part by the voices of singers of flamenco. You could almost, but not quite, think of him as a troubadour. He also wrote poems about his guitar weeping (before George Harrison did) and, in another poem, asks to be buried with it.

"Confronted by the real object, my first impression was that there was something toylike about it. It seemed altogether in keeping with an owner who could easily access the dreamy, diminutive world of childhood games and songs. At the end of my poem, I inject a bit of fantasy by imagining a young museum guard coming and picking up the guitar. It was my way of wanting to extend some warmth toward Lorca. In reality, there was no guard around when I saw the show—and a good thing too. Photographs were not permitted. Ordinarily, I comply with such prohibitions, but emboldened by my love of Lorca, I simply couldn't resist taking one. It's a nice souvenir of my stolen moment alone with his guitar."

GERALD FLEMING was born in San Francisco in 1946. His five books of poetry are *The Bastard and the Bishop* (Hanging Loose Press, 2021), *One* (an experiment in monosyllabic prose poems; Hanging Loose, 2016), *The Choreographer* (Sixteen Rivers Press, 2013), *Night of Pure Breathing* (Hanging Loose, 2011), and *Swimmer Climbing onto Shore* (Sixteen

Rivers, 2005). During the final five years of the twentieth century he edited and published the literary magazine *Barnabe Mountain Review*; he has also edited *The Collected Poetry and Prose of Lawrence Fixel* (Sixteen Rivers, 2020), the vitreous magazine *One (More) Glass*, and the epistolary magazine *Forward to Velma*. For thirty-seven years, Fleming taught in San Francisco's public schools. He lives most of the year in California, part of the year in Paris. He doesn't apply for fellowships, awards, or grants, but when he turns eighty, he intends to begin doing so.

Of "Two Thousand," Fleming writes: "My wife and I have been married a very long time. I must admit to one bright Sunday morning wondering how many times over those years we'd made love, was amused by the nature of that thought, then wondered further whether there were men who actually *did* count—obsessive in that way; that thought widened to the realization that if he counted lovemaking, he damned well probably counted other things too. But I wanted the poem to focus less on the man's nuttiness/obsession and more on his wife's reaction: *her* chain of thought—*she's* the important character here, and irresolution is important to the end."

JOANNA FUHRMAN was born in Brooklyn in 1972. An assistant teaching professor in creative writing at Rutgers University, she is the author of seven books of poetry: *Data Mind* (Curbstone/Northwestern University Press, 2024), *To a New Era* (Hanging Loose Press, 2021), *The Year of Yellow Butterflies* (Hanging Loose, 2015), *Pageant* (Alice James Books, 2009), *Moraine* (Hanging Loose, 2006), *Ugh Ugh Ocean* (Hanging Loose, 2006), and *Freud in Brooklyn* (Hanging Loose, 2000).

Fuhrman writes: "'How to Change the Filter on the Developing Cell Matter in Your Womb' was written to be part of *Data Mind*, my book of darkly comic, surreal, feminist prose poems about digital life from the perspective of a non-digital native. One thread in the collection is the viewing of pre-internet films through the frame of internet-era tropes. Another is the siloing effect of social media, and how this leads people to see political issues (like reproductive health) vastly differently. What happens to older films when they are mixed up with the chaos of online spaces? Does the present leak into the past? And when everyone is living in a different genre of experience, what happens to what we used to think of as reality? The approach of this poem is lighthearted, but my heart is also broken."

AMY GERSTLER was born in San Diego, California, in 1956. *Is This My Final Form?* (2025) and *Index of Women* (2021) are her most recent books of poems, both published by Penguin Random House. She is currently collaborating with composer/actor Steve Gunderson on a musical. In 2019, she received a Foundation for Contemporary Arts C.D. Wright Grant. In 2018, she won a Guggenheim Fellowship. Her book *Dearest Creature* (Penguin, 2009) was named a *New York Times* Notable Book. She was the guest editor of *The Best American Poetry 2010.*

Of "Postcard," Gerstler writes: "Francesca Gabbiani, a terrific artist, asked me to write text for a small exhibition catalog of her luminous images of cacti. If you want a peek at that body of her work, visit the Baert Gallery's website. I am always looking for excuses to write about altered states, so I was gleeful remembering peyote is a cactus and therefore I could use it in one of the poems for the cactus project. I ended up writing a suite of other poems for that catalog. This one didn't make it into the publication. It didn't turn out as cactus-centric as I had planned, swerving into other territories, as poems will do, though I did attempt to steer it back to peyote at the end."

JAMES ALLEN HALL (he/they) was born in Columbus, Indiana, in 1976. They are the author of two books of poetry and a book of lyric personal essays: *Now You're the Enemy* (University of Arkansas Press, 2008), *I Liked You Better Before I Knew You So Well* (CSU Poetry Center, 2017), and *Romantic Comedy* (Four Way Books, 2023). They have received awards and fellowships from Lambda Literary, the National Endowment for the Arts, the Civitella Ranieri Foundation, the Bread Loaf Writers' Conference, the Maryland State Arts Council, the University of Arizona Poetry Center, and the Fellowship of Southern Writers. They teach at Washington College, where they direct the Rose O'Neill Literary House. With Aaron Smith, James cohosts *Breaking Form: A Poetry and Culture Podcast.* You can find them online at www.jamesallenhall.com.

Of "Inheritance at Corresponding Periods of Life, at Corresponding Seasons of the Year, as Limited by Sex," Hall writes: "The zoological data in the poem are imagined, fictionalized, or merely accidentally correct. The autobiographical data in the poem are true (inasmuch as memory is documentary). The poem angles imagined and autobiographical inheritances toward each other to make a self-portrait of perception."

JEFFREY HARRISON was born in 1957, in Cincinnati, Ohio (also the hometown of Kenneth Koch, the subject of his poem in this volume). Harrison's six books of poetry include *The Singing Underneath* (Dutton, 1988), a National Poetry Series winner; *Into Daylight* (Tupelo Press, 2014), winner of the Dorset Prize; and *Between Lakes* (Four Way Books, 2020), selected as a 2021 Must-Read Book by the Massachusetts Center for the Book. His poems have appeared in three previous editions of *The Best American Poetry*. He has received fellowships from the Guggenheim Foundation, the National Endowment for the Arts, and the Bogliasco Foundation. His poems have been translated into Bulgarian, Italian, Norwegian, and Portuguese.

Of "Amnesia," Harrison writes: "I don't remember anything about writing this poem. Just kidding—I remember everything. And everything that happens in the poem really happened: having the dream, searching for the phantom Koch poem titled 'Amnesia,' and even finding, online, the John Kinsella poem bearing that title and (incredibly) dedicated to Kenneth Koch. That sequence of events exhilarated me in much the same way that reading Koch's poetry often does, propelling me through the first draft.

"As a freshman at Columbia in 1976–77, I took Koch's yearlong 'Imaginative Writing' class (he didn't like the term *creative writing*). Of the twelve students in the class, four of us went on to publish books of poetry—the other three are Stephen Ackerman, Jessica Greenbaum, and Daniel Meltz—and we've remained friends ever since. It was a thrill to be in a classroom with Koch, who, among other things, could speak fluently off the top of his head in sestinas, pantoums, or ottava rima.

"In the late nineties, when I was teaching at Phillips Academy, Kenneth came to Andover to do a reading and meet the student writers. I had the pleasure and honor of introducing his reading and hanging out with him during his visit. At that point he seemed like the youngest seventy-three-year-old in the history of the world. Sadly, he would only live a few more years.

"Not long after the poem was published, the composer Scott Wheeler, who studied with Koch's friend and collaborator Virgil Thomson, set it to music, and the song recently had its premiere—serendipitous timing, since 2025 is Kenneth Koch's centenary."

ROBERT HASS was born in San Francisco in 1941. His most recent book is a translation: *Czesław Miłosz, Poet in the New World: Poems, 1946–1953*, edited and translated by Robert Hass and David Frick (Ecco, 2025). Hass was guest editor of *The Best American Poetry 2001*.

Hass writes: "I think 'A Sunset' speaks for itself, or tries to."

BOB HICOK was born in Grand Ledge, Michigan, in 1960. His most recent book is *Water Look Away* (Copper Canyon Press, 2023).

Born in metro Detroit in 1990 and currently residing in Novi, Michigan, NAZIFA ISLAM is the author of the poetry collections *Searching for a Pulse* (Whitepoint Press, 2013) and *Forlorn Light: Virginia Woolf Found Poems* (Shearsman Books, 2021). She earned her MFA from Oregon State University.

Islam writes: "I wrote 'The Wind Whipped Tears into My Eyes' in December 2022 while in Paris to attend a concert featuring Belgian composer Alexandre Jamar's song adaptation of 'Psyche,' another of my Sylvia Plath found poems. The poem was written using only the words from one paragraph of *The Unabridged Journals of Sylvia Plath*—I didn't allow myself to repeat words, add words, or edit the language for tense or any other consideration. I spent a week in Paris and made a point of writing a handful of Sylvia Plath found poems while I was there. Those four poems ended up rounding off my collection of over seventy Sylvia Plath found poems."

Born in Toronto in 1967, HENRY ISRAELI is the author of four poetry collections, most recently *Our Age of Anxiety* (White Pine Press, 2019) and *god's breath hovering across the waters* (Four Way Books, 2016), and editor of *Lords of Misrule: 20 Years of Saturnalia Books* (Saturnalia, 2022). He is also the translator of three critically acclaimed books by Albanian poet Luljeta Lleshanaku. Henry Israeli is also the founder and editor of Saturnalia Books and teaches in the English and philosophy department of Drexel University, where he runs the annual Drexel Writing Festival and the Jewish studies program.

Of "Escape Artists," Israeli writes: "Every Jew, in some way, has a plan to hide or escape—whether it's their physical self or their Jewish identity. And hiding, for Jews, is a spectrum. Sometimes it's tucking in a Star of David pendant, sometimes it's conveniently not identifying one's last name, sometimes it's avoiding unwelcoming areas on a college campus, and sometimes it means literally hiding in mortal fear or crossing borders in the middle of the night. 'Escape Artists' is a poem from a collection in progress, *Between the Trees*, which focuses on intergenerational trauma, particularly in children of Holocaust survivors, such as myself. One of the dominant and recurring themes in reaction to the perpetual cycle of anti-Semitism everywhere in the world is the instinctive drive to survive. This poem addresses the different layers of escaping, and Harry Houdini seemed like a perfect conduit to carry that complexity. In the end, death is the only sure escape, but the act of escaping itself is eternally repeated from generation to generation: It never dies. This poem was written before October 7, but appeared shortly afterward, imbued with fresh meaning."

FATIMA JAFAR was born in Karachi, Pakistan, in 1999. She studied comparative literature at University College London and received her MFA in creative writing from Emerson College. Fatima now lives in California, where she is a first-year Wallace Stegner Fellow in poetry.

Of "In the End of the Beginning of Our Lives," Jafar writes: "This poem was written for a dear friend, and for a time in our lives when we were much younger. Growing up, we spent almost every minute together, and this poem attempts to catalog that fierce connection, as well as the seemingly endless nature of time that seems to only exist in childhood. There is also so much sadness in girlhood, and I wanted to touch upon the advent of insecurity, desire, and self-image as well."

BRIONNE JANAE is a poet and teaching artist living in Brooklyn with their two dogs. They are the author of *Because You Were Mine* (Haymarket Books, 2023); *Blessed Are the Peacemakers* (2021), which won the 2020 Cave Canem Northwestern University Press Poetry Prize; and *After Jubilee* (BOAAT Press, 2017). Brionne is a 2023 NEA Creative Writing Fellow, a Hedgebrook Alum, and a proud Cave Canem Fellow. Off the page, they go by Breezy.

RAPHAEL JENKINS prefers to go by Ralph, as he was born in 1990 and has heard every Ninja Turtle joke ever uttered. He is a native of Detroit, Michigan, currently residing in Kentucky with his Boo-thang and their eight-year-old boy. A chef by day and an essayist, poet, and screenwriter in his dreams, he, like Issa Rae, is rooting for everybody Black.

Of "Two men too man to mourn," Jenkins writes: "That day, while my friend and I were feeling our feelings, we were laughed at. Made to feel small for our willingness to show our hurt. Even at a funeral, a man must be a man, despite his heart lying in pieces on the floor. I began writing this poem four or five years ago, mostly because I needed to think through my heartbreak, also because those cackling hens hurt my feelings. In lieu of a poem that immortalized the assholes who mocked us, I wanted to question the logic we employed to convince ourselves to run away. What began as a would-be clapback turned into a balm for me. A reminder that the pains of life are numerous, unavoidable, and, often, more than enough reason to cry. This poem was written in loving memory of Loleatha Smith. Thank you for teaching me how to sing."

VIRGINIA KONCHAN was born in Cleveland, Ohio, in 1979. She is the author of five poetry collections—*Requiem* (Carnegie Mellon University Press, 2025), *Bel Canto* (Carnegie Mellon, 2022), *Hallelujah Time* (Véhicule Press, 2021), *Any God Will Do* (Carnegie Mellon, 2020), and *The End of Spectacle* (Carnegie Mellon, 2018)—as well as a short story collection, *Anatomical Gift* (Noctuary Press, 2017). Coeditor of *Marbles on the Floor: How to Assemble a Book of Poems* (University of Akron Press, 2023), and recipient of fellowships from the Amy Clampitt Poet Residency Program and the National Endowment for the Humanities, she holds a PhD from the Program for Writers at the University of Illinois Chicago.

Of "Miraculous," Konchan writes: "I've memorized many of the Psalms as devotional practice; their invocatory rhetoric and cadence captivate me and have led me into the study of ancient Hebrew poetry and the use of chiastic parallelism as a literary device (akin to Jesus's use of parables). Psalms of protection (23, 91, 121) are especially meaningful to me, allaying my anxiety and grief over personal and world events that otherwise would have taken a foothold. King David, a chief psalmist, was repeatedly delivered from his enemies and death, making music of lamentation, battle, and victory. 'Miraculous' is a praise poem, from the other side."

VICTORIA KORNICK was born in Alexandria, Virginia, in 1991. She holds an MFA from New York University, where she was a Rona Jaffe and Goldwater Hospital Fellow, and has received support from the Elizabeth George Foundation, the Oak Spring Garden Foundation, the Community of Writers, and the Saltonstall Foundation for the Arts. She lives in Los Angeles, where she is a PhD candidate in creative nonfiction at the University of Southern California.

Kornick writes: "'Eileen' comes from a manuscript of poetry about close girlhood friendships and their aftermath. I wrote this poem after attending a talk by the photographer Rachel Larsen Weaver on (among other things) Sally Mann's *At Twelve* photographs. It's a series of images I've been returning to since I was a teenager myself—images of adolescence that hold a dangerous tension between power and powerlessness. The subjects, all twelve-year-old girls, look frankly at the camera as the world around them turns sinister and mysterious: the word *DOOM* scrawled on the dusty hood of a car, stockings and bloodstained bedding on a clothesline, older men lurking too close for comfort.

"Rachel's talk sent me back to these photographs, and I thought about how my friends and I taught one another things—so often, incorrect things—as teenagers, and how humor, curiosity, and anxiety ran alongside one another as we tried to understand what we desired. I wrote this poem imagining Mann's subjects in *At Twelve* a few years later, as my own friends at sixteen, impressing, warning, judging, and misunderstanding one another, repeating and testing what we'd been told. It was a time when language seemed pliable, even deceptive, as we made each other laugh with double entendres, and also spent hours studying SAT flashcards.

"I remember, too, sitting in a theater rehearsal that year, reading a copy of *The Best American Poetry 2007* I'd gotten from our school library, and trying to convince my friends to read some of the poems. That version of myself, the one who became the speaker of this poem, would be astonished about how the future would turn out."

Born in Tennessee in 1983, MARIANNE KUNKEL is the author of *Hillary, Made Up* (Stephen F. Austin State University Press, 2018) and *The Laughing Game* (Finishing Line Press, 2012). She is an associate professor of English at Johnson County Community College. She holds an MFA in poetry from the University of Florida and a PhD in English from the University of Nebraska–Lincoln, where she was the managing editor of *Prairie Schooner* and the African Poetry Book Fund. She is the co-editor-in-chief of *Kansas City Review*. She loves writing poems and baking pies, and she posts images of both on Instagram at @asliceofpoetry.

Of "Apostate Abecedarian," Kunkel writes: "This poem emerged from a midlife project to reapproach my childhood in the Mormon faith through a compassionately curious, woman-centered lens. The poem is part of a manuscript that spotlights and celebrates women mentioned in the Book of Mormon; only six women are named, so I had to be resourceful and add poems about living Mormon women who have influenced me. An early draft of this poem was entitled 'Braver Than Me,' springing from my intention to pay tribute to my cousin and sister who rebelled within the church. What elevated and saved this poem, as happens so often in my writing process, is poetic form; the abecedarian, a form with which I hadn't experimented before writing this, enabled me to organize images and conjure pop culture references I wouldn't have thought of had I not been searching for words starting with *w*, *x*, and so forth. The alphabet I learned in childhood became the portal through which I reconsidered a more mature religious text."

MICHAEL LALLY was born in Orange, New Jersey, in 1942, the youngest of seven in an Irish American clan of cops, politicians, musicians, and a Franciscan friar. He began civil rights activism and poetry readings in 1959 and enlisted in the US Air Force from 1962 to 1966, after which he attended the University of Iowa on the GI Bill. He ran for sheriff of Johnson County, Iowa, on the Peace and Freedom Party ticket in 1968. He has been an activist for women's and gay rights from 1969 to the present. The most recent of his thirty books since 1970 include *Another Way to Play: Poems 1960–2017* (Seven Stories Press, 2018) and *Say It Again: An Autobiography in Sonnets* (Beltway Editions, 2024). He was awarded National Endowment for the Arts Poetry Fellowships in 1974 and 1981 (the latter denounced in Congress by Republicans citing the poem "My Life" as "pornography" in an attempt to defund the NEA), the 1997 PEN Oakland/Josephine Miles Literary Award for Excellence in Literature for *Cant Be Wrong*

(Coffee House Press, 1997), and a 2000 American Book Award for *It's Not Nostalgia: Poetry & Prose* (Black Sparrow Press, 1999). From 1966 to 1984 he reviewed books for *The Washington Post* and *The Village Voice*. From 1979 to 2009 he worked as a scriptwriter and actor on television shows and films including *NYPD Blue*, *Deadwood*, *Drugstore Cowboy*, and *White Fang*. He writes the blog *Lally's Alley*.

Of "DC 1972," Lally writes: "In the 1960s I wrote a series of twenty sonnets as a mini-autobiography of my first twenty years, called *The South Orange Sonnets*, which won me the NYC 92nd Street Y Poetry Center's Discovery Award in 1972. I've been filling in the rest of the story with more location sonnets ever since. The three selected here were constructed from journal entries from 1972 when I was beginning my thirties while living in Washington, DC, and discovering whole new ways of experiencing life."

Danusha Laméris is a poet and essayist born in Cambridge, Massachusetts, to a Dutch father and Barbadian mother, and raised in northern California. *The Moons of August* (Autumn House, 2014), her first book, was chosen by Naomi Shihab Nye as the winner of the Autumn House Press Poetry Prize. She is also the author of *Bonfire Opera* (University of Pittsburgh Press, 2020), winner of the 2021 Northern California Book Award. Her third book, *Blade by Blade*, was published in 2024 by Copper Canyon Press. Laméris is on the faculty of Pacific University's low-residency MFA program.

Of "Second Sight," Laméris writes: "Most of us carry stories that cycle through on repeat: We tell the same tales from year to year, perhaps with different details or embellishments. The stories in this poem are familiar to those who took part in them, and were familiar enough to me as to find them too ordinary for art. But I started writing this as a kind of tribute to my high school and college companions who put up with each other's (and my) eccentricities as gracefully as they did. That in itself seemed a kind of art. And so did survival. Given the history of anyone's ancestral line, it's a miracle each of us is here at all. The terrible is always taking place, with or without warning. And yet there was always at least one person in our lineage who outran the tsunami, survived on scant grains of rice, lived through the coldest winter—sometimes, long enough to tell about it."

HAILEY LEITHAUSER is the author of *Swoop* (Graywolf Press, 2013), which won the Poetry Foundation's Emily Dickinson First Book Award and the Towson Prize for Literature, and *Saint Worm* (Able Muse Press, 2019). This is her fourth appearance in *The Best American Poetry*, which has left her feeling quite full of herself.

Leithauser writes: "'Five Postcards' came from the scraps of several unfinished poems that had been nagging at me for years. The first was an attempt at a blessing poem made of clichés—May your life be a bowl of cherries; May the world be your oyster—which just couldn't seem to get off the ground, and at some point got tangled in with a poem about a lounge singer (and yes, the grammatical mistake in that line about the piano is intentional). The brevity of these two bits mashed up together brought to mind Ted Kooser's collection of postcard poems to Jim Harrison, and I finally saw the poem's proper form. I went back through my files and found fragments of a couple of other yearning poems, and threw in a story a woman told me about having a drunken argument with her girlfriend on the way back to their hotel one night, which ended up with them finding an unlocked garage and doing it on the hood of some stranger's car. Some more twiddling and tweaking, and the poem eventually tamped itself down into the length and shape of a postcard, with 'whole world' meant to dangle as a salutation at the end. It was a lot of fun and a lot of work to write, and 'Plump & Deciduous, Smirched Girly Girl' remains one of my favorite endearments to this day."

AMIT MAJMUDAR was born in New York City in 1979. His recent books include *Twin A: A Memoir* (Slant Books, 2023), *The Great Game: Essays on Poetics* (Acre Books, 2024), and *Three Metamorphoses* (Orison Books, 2025). A new poetry collection is forthcoming from Knopf in 2026.

Of "Patronage," Majmudar writes: "I've always wanted to write and read all day, for all my days. This plan was complicated early on by a stubbornly recurrent discomfort in my abdomen called hunger, and the fact that rain and snow interfered with my concentration and ruined my books. I had to figure out a way to feed and shelter this needy, nerve-ridden appendage, my body. My problem was compounded when four additional people crowded my ascetic literary solitude, and I found my appendage appended to a family.

"So, pouring ashes on my head, gnashing my teeth, I got a job. Finding no one willing to pay me a living wage for staring at the wall above my computer screen, I became a radiologist. Radiology reports are the opposite of poems, and not just because they're in prose: People actually pay for them. Too much poetic license can get your medical license revoked.

"Many a practicing poet is stuck being his or her own Maecenas. I don't know about you, but I wouldn't mind hitching myself to a patron, however shady—'money doesn't smell,' as the old Romans used to say. Alas, not even one of our nefarious capitalist titans is interested in owning a poet.

"If 'money is a kind of poetry,' as Wallace Stevens once said, it stands to reason that poetry is a kind of money: the *air* in *billionaire*, horizon-sized zeroes forgetting to start with a one."

CHRIS MASON was born in Massachusetts in 1952 but grew up in Minnesota. He is a member of two bands—Old Songs, who translate Archaic Greek poetry and put it to music, and the Tinklers, who recorded three LPs for Shimmy Disc in the eighties and nineties. Old Songs can be heard at PennSound, and the Tinklers can be heard on Bandcamp. Mason's books of poetry are *Poems of a Doggy* (Pod Books, 1977), *Hum Who Hiccup* (Narrow House, 2011), *Something Something Morning* (Blabbermouth Press, 2020), and *Of Rare Earths* (UnCollected Press, 2024). He is retired after thirty-one years as a Baltimore City Schools special educator. He lives in Baltimore with his wife, Ann, and three chickens: Mars, Our Lady, and Thorleif.

Mason writes: "'Well Water' uses a two-word line, which I first encountered in Louis Zukofsky's beautiful 'A-19.' My series of poems using the two-word line is called 'Clomp Clomp.' These poems were mostly written immediately after waking, from a night's sleep or after a nap, using images from the wonderful 'hypnopompic' state in which dreams, memories, and sensations swarm in one's mind. Test patterns were what you saw if you left your TV on late at night after all the programming was finished. Siegfried was a local cartoon character in Minnesota who arrived in a spaceship and shot a flag out of a gun with the words 'Look There!' printed on the flag. I thought it said 'Time for another cartoon,' but my older brother John, who knew how to read, told me it said 'Look There!' and I did."

GREG MCBRIDE was born on March 2, 1945, in San Diego, California, at a wartime army camp on the grounds of what is now the Torrey Pines golf course. After growing up in a military family, he went to college at Princeton, then served in the army for four years, including one year as a photographer in the Vietnam War. After graduating from Georgetown Law, he practiced law in DC for thirty years before beginning to write poems. Soon enough, he decided to retire and spend his remaining years in poetry. In 2005, he founded *Innisfree Poetry Journal*, which he continues to edit. At sixty-seven, he won *Boulevard*'s Emerging Poets Prize. His two full-length collections are *Porthole* (Liam Rector First Book Prize for Poetry; Briery Creek Press, 2012) and *Guest of Time* (Pond Road Press, 2023).

Of "Know Thyself," McBride writes: "I'm a small man, not quite 5'4" and 120 pounds, but I played baseball, football, basketball, and eventually became a Pennsylvania state wrestling champion in high school. I've not minded being small, but recently decided to see what sort of poems that subject might produce. A few poems have come of it: 'Paul Simon and I,' 'Sizes,' and, most recently, 'Know Thyself,' which unveils an attitude of indifferent awareness (my wrists are so small that, as a matter of course, I look for women's wristwatches that might work for me). Despite size's occasional inconvenience, I did manage to pair up with a very pretty, smart girl for the past fifty years. When we met, I was wearing a three-piece pin-striped suit. I later learned that she had confided to a friend, 'What a silly little man.'"

JILL MCDONOUGH was born in Hartford, Connecticut, in 1972. Her books of poems include *American Treasure* (Alice James Books, 2022), *Here All Night* (Alice James, 2019), *Reaper* (Alice James, 2017), *Where You Live* (Salt, 2012), and *Habeas Corpus* (Salt, 2008). The recipient of fellowships from the Lannan Foundation and the NEA, she teaches in the MFA program at UMass Boston.

Of "What We Are For," McDonough writes: "My friend Billy Sothern hanged himself and I guess I'm always going to be messed up about that. Also, isn't it amazing to be alive and not incarcerated or quarantined? So you can go to the post office and the library and the wine store? It is!"

JOYELLE MCSWEENEY was born in Boston in 1976. She is the author of ten books of poetry, prose, criticism, and translation, from her debut collection, *The Red Bird*, winner of the inaugural Fence Modern Poets Prize in 2001, to *Dead Youth, or, The Leaks* (Litmus Press, 2014), a verse play, which won the first Leslie Scalapino Award for Innovative Women Playwrights, to *The Necropastoral*, a widely read work of decadent eco-poetics, which appeared in the University of Michigan Press *Poets on Poetry* series in 2011, to her most recent poetry volumes, *Toxicon and Arachne* (2020) and *Death Styles* (2024), both from Nightboat Books. A Guggenheim Fellow and winner of the Shelley Memorial Award from the Poetry Society of America, McSweeney is cofounder of the international press Action Books and teaches at Notre Dame.

Of "Death Styles 5/6/2021: *Terminator 2*, Late Style," McSweeney writes: "After our baby died, I cursed Spring for returning without her. I cursed myself, of course, and I also cursed away my poetry: Having written a book about her loss, I snapped shut my laptop and swore, *No more*. And like all poet's curses, it held. A few years later, I realized I was barely surviving, though I had to, for my living children's sake. All I could think of to keep myself on the planet was to start writing again. But how to begin?

"I set myself three rules: 1) to write every day, 2) to accept any inspiration that came my way, no matter how absurd or inconsequential, and 3) to write until that inspiration was completely exhausted. To my surprise, this formula worked, and became the book called *Death Styles*. I learned to live with death, and in doing so, I wrote myself back to life.

"This particular Death Style takes as its inspiration *Terminator 2* and the idea of 'late style,' the notion that an artist might achieve a certain chiaroscuro or muscularity in the final phase of their work. The poem thinks about whether I am entering a 'late style,' whether I am late in the plot of my life. It wonders what I can still do for my dead and living daughters, as the planet enters its terminal phase. It gets stuck on the muscularity of the mother figure in *T2*, which was exceptionally noteworthy at the time, even upstaging Arnold's, and it rearranges all my memories of that movie around that actress's physical strength. Finally, it takes on my old nemesis: Spring."

ANGE MLINKO is the author of seven poetry collections, most recently *Foxglovewise* (Farrar, Straus and Giroux, 2025). Her study of modernist poets in Florida, *Difficult Ornaments* (Oxford University Press), came out in 2023. She lives in Gainesville, Florida, and teaches in the MFA program at the University of Florida. She received a Guggenheim Fellowship in 2014.

Mlinko writes: "'The Bougainvillea Line' is partly an ode to the shrub that marks, at least to me, the latitude of the tropics—also the attitude of the tropics! From an ode it segues into the fantasy of the perfect community enabled by the natural abundance and benevolence of the environment. It's simple. I wish I could live in this poem."

NICHOLAS MONTEMARANO was born in Brooklyn in 1970. He is the author of five books, most recently a memoir, *If There Are Any Heavens* (Persea Books, 2022), and a novel, *The Senator's Children* (Tin House Books, 2017). The recipient of a National Endowment for the Arts Fellowship, he is the Alumni Professor of creative writing and belles lettres at Franklin & Marshall College in Lancaster, Pennsylvania.

Of "A Neighborly Day in This Beautywood," Montemarano writes: "This poem exists because I forgot my Nextdoor password. While Nextdoor continued to send daily emails announcing recent posts, I was given access only to the first 75 characters, followed by '. . . See more.' What I saw were the beginnings of rants, pleas, warnings, complaints, threats, apologies, advice. Fragments. Unfinished thoughts. A collective voice. The poem's title is from the song 'Won't You Be My Neighbor?' by Fred Rogers."

YEHOSHUA NOVEMBER was born in Miami Beach, Florida, in 1979. He is the author of three books of poetry, *God's Optimism* (Main Street Rag, 2010), *Two Worlds Exist* (2016), and *The Concealment of Endless Light* (2024), the latter two from Orison Books. He teaches creative writing at Rutgers University and Touro University.

Of "What About the Here and Now?" November writes: "Yevtushenko writes, 'A poet's autobiography is his poetry.' Comprised of vignettes and interwoven sections, this poem explores the precipitous transitions and surprising juxtapositions that have characterized my life thus far. Fittingly, part of the poem was written during a stopover at O'Hare Airport on a return trip from Postville, Iowa, to Newark,

New Jersey. Another section was written in an office that once served as an oil tank closet. I'm honored that Apollinaire, Szymborska, Kafka, the Baal Shem Tov, my wife, son, and father all make appearances."

SHARON OLDS was born in San Francisco in 1942. She has written thirteen books of poetry, including *Balladz* (Knopf, 2022). *Stag's Leap* (Knopf, 2012) received the Pulitzer Prize and England's T. S. Eliot Prize. Olds holds the Erich Maria Remarque Chair at New York University's graduate program in creative writing, where she helped to found workshop programs for residents of Coler-Goldwater Hospital and for veterans of the Iraq and Afghanistan wars.

MICHAEL ONDAATJE was born in Sri Lanka in 1943. In 1962 he moved to Canada. He is the author of several novels, books of poetry, a memoir, and a nonfiction book on film editing. His works include *The English Patient*, *In the Skin of a Lion*, *Anil's Ghost*, *Divisadero*, *The Cat's Table*, and *Warlight*. His latest book of poetry, *A Year of Last Things*, was published in 2024 by M&S (Canada) and Knopf (US). He lives in Toronto.

Born in 1975 in Cork, Ireland, PÁDRAIG Ó TUAMA presents *Poetry Unbound* from On Being Studios and has published two anthologies with W. W. Norton from that podcast. In early 2025 Copper Canyon Press published *Kitchen Hymns*, his fourth poetry collection. A freelance artist, he is poet-in-residence with the Morton Deutsch International Center for Cooperation and Conflict Resolution at Columbia University. He splits his time between Belfast and New York City.

Ó Tuama writes: "I am interested in questions of God, although I'm nervous about belief. 'Do You Believe in God?' is part of a sequence from the book *Kitchen Hymns*. (*Kitchen hymns* is a term from Ireland for traditional holy songs disallowed from being sung in the chapel because they were in the Irish language, not Latin.) When considering the question 'Do you believe in God?' I am interested in a tangible response to an abstract question. So an answer emerges as a story: memories of a belonging and escape; nostalgia; animals I've loved; erotics, exile, and engagement. Placing the poem in small stanzas that veer between opposite sides of the page is a play on binary imaginations that one either does or doesn't believe in God. For me, the poem's intuition exists in the empty space between the stanzas."

JOSE PADUA was born in Washington, DC, in 1957. After college, he worked for a decade as a research assistant at the Library of Congress, then left for New York City. His record of employment has been spotty ever since. After returning to his hometown and spending a couple of decades there and in Virginia's Shenandoah Valley, he and his wife (the poet Heather L. Davis) and children have moved slightly north to Lancaster, Pennsylvania. His first book, *A Short History of Monsters*, was chosen by Billy Collins as the winner of the 2019 Miller Williams Poetry Prize and is out from the University of Arkansas Press.

Of "Godzilla Meets the Beast," Padua writes: "This is from my recently completed sequence of sixty-nine sonnets, and as with many of the poems therein, it attempts to connect things one might not normally try to connect. Here, it's so-called highbrow and lowbrow, twerking and late capitalism, Godzilla and Stephen Crane (specifically his famous poem in which the speaker happens upon a beast in the desert), Godzilla and James Joyce (that the snow extends 'to the outer suburbs' is meant to recall the snow that is 'general all over Ireland' in 'The Dead'), and so on. All this in my efforts to present a poetry that is something of an agnostic leap of faith that simultaneously lifts you and makes you go *WTF?*"

ELISE PASCHEN, an enrolled member of the Osage Nation, is the author of six poetry collections, most recently *Tallchief* (Magic City Books, 2023) and *Blood Wolf Moon* (Red Hen Press, 2025). She has edited or coedited numerous anthologies, including *The Eloquent Poem* (Persea Books, 2019) and the *New York Times* bestseller *Poetry Speaks* (Sourcebooks, 2001). Born in Chicago in 1959, Dr. Paschen teaches in the MFA writing program at the School of the Art Institute of Chicago.

Of "After *Killers of the Flower Moon*," Paschen writes: "Over the years, I have been haunted by a tragic period of our history, the Reign of Terror (1921–1926), when outsiders murdered the Osage for their oil headrights. My persona poem, '*Wi'-gi-e*' (from *Bestiary*, Red Hen Press, 2009), is spoken by Mollie Burkhart, whose family was systematically killed during this time in Fairfax, Oklahoma. A line from '*Wi'-gi-e*' inspired the title for both David Grann's book and Martin Scorsese's movie.

"I was moved to watch the Osage Nation premiere of *Killers of the Flower Moon* and then to meet the actress, Lily Gladstone, who brings Mollie Burkhart to life. The story Lily told me about wearing my great-grandmother Eliza Tall Chief's blankets in the film continued to resonate. In my notebook, several months later, I jotted: 'How can we re-embody our ancestors through the clothes they wore, the objects they held?' The poem 'After *Killers of the Flower Moon*' is a centerpiece in my new collection, *Blood Wolf Moon* (Red Hen Press, 2025), a book that grapples with this dark period of American history."

ALISON PELEGRIN, Louisiana's Poet Laureate for 2023–2025, was born in New Orleans in 1972 and is a lifelong resident of the state. Her most recent poetry collections are *Our Lady of Bewilderment* (2022), which won the Phillip H. McMath Post Publication Book Award in Poetry, and *Waterlines* (2016), both with LSU Press, and, with the University of Akron Press, *Hurricane Party* (2011) and *Big Muddy River of Stars* (2007), which won the Akron Poetry Prize. She has received grants from the National Endowment for the Arts, the Louisiana Division of the Arts, the Foundation for Louisiana, and the Louisiana Board of Regents. A 2024 Poet Laureate Fellowship from the Academy of American Poets will support her poetry outreach in Louisiana prisons and community centers. For more than twenty years, she has taught at Southeastern Louisiana University.

Of "Zero Bothers Given," Pelegrin writes: "I used to lift weights. I used to trek for miles with a forty-pound sandbag on my shoulders. I competed in a Tough Mudder and used the finish line photo as a Christmas card. My black sandbag with handles and a zillion pockets also had a spot for a morale patch, and in that spot, instead of an American flag, or 'Embrace the Suck,' I affixed a 'Zero Bothers Given' Winnie-the-Pooh patch. Pooh just skips along, red half-shirt, no pants. Tra-la-la. It cracks me up. It should come as no surprise that I injured myself and abruptly quit all of these activities, but I have been tripping over that sandbag on the floor in my garage and laughing at that patch for years. I have become one with the message of the patch: I am over it. And my tramp stamp is still in need of a footnote."

DONALD PLATT was born in Coral Gables, Florida, in 1957. His eighth book of poetry, *Swansdown*, won the Off the Grid Poetry Prize and was published in 2022 by Grid Books, which will publish his next book, *Tender Voyeur*, in the fall of 2025. He has been awarded two individual artist fellowships from the NEA. He teaches at Purdue University. "Streak" is the fourth of his poems to be published in *The Best American Poetry*.

Platt writes: "'Streak' exists because I saw that glittering river run of spilled feed corn on State Route 231 outside of West Lafayette, Indiana. A week before, I had read a short profile of Robert Opel in Michael Schulman's article 'Ballad of the Oscar Streaker,' which appeared in the February 6, 2023, issue of *The New Yorker*. All that was left for me to do was free-associate to the Rodgers and Hammerstein tune 'A Wonderful Guy' to connect the two. I love 'walking into' poems. In this case, I drove past a poem. It was also great fun to research 'Streak' by watching the video of the 1974 Academy Awards on YouTube and to capture frame by frame, word for word, how David Niven came up with his bon mot. Humor should, I believe, play a more intrinsic part in our poetry. I'd like to add that this poem is not mine alone. As the Beatles have it on *Sgt. Pepper's Lonely Hearts Club Band*, I 'get by' and metaphorically 'high with a little help from my friends.' The brilliant poet Bruce Beasley suggested crucial cuts to 'Streak,' which made it more streamlined."

Born in 1975 in Ostrava, in the former Czechoslovakia, JANA PRIKRYL grew up in Canada from the age of six and moved to New York City in her late twenties. She is the author of three poetry collections: *The After Party* (Tim Duggan Books, 2016), *No Matter* (Tim Duggan, 2019), and *Midwood* (W. W. Norton, 2022). She has received an award in literature from the American Academy of Arts and Letters as well as fellowships from the Guggenheim Foundation, the Radcliffe Institute for Advanced Study, and the Jan Michalski Foundation. She works as an editor at *The New York Review of Books*.

Born in Denver, Colorado, in 1961, ELIZABETH ROBINSON has published several books of poetry, including *Pure Descent* (Green Integer Press, 2002), a winner of the National Poetry Series, and *Apprehend* (Apogee Press / Fence Books, 2003), a winner of the Fence Modern Poets Prize.

Of "The Extinct World," Robinson writes: "I was in Mendocino,

California, soaking in the beauty and seeming bounty of the environment there at the same time I was reading news of droughts, fires, and accelerating plant and animal extinctions. The loss hit me and felt unbearable. I felt grief for our transforming planet and, in particular, for the sense of pervasive disappearance: for the emptying world that now confronts my sons."

MATTHEW ROHRER is the author of eleven books of poems, most recently *Army of Giants* (2024), *The Sky Contains the Plans* (2020), and *The Others* (2017), which won *The Believer* Book Award, all published by Wave Books. He was a cofounder of *Fence Magazine* and Fence Books, and teaches at New York University. He is a proud citizen of Brooklyn.

Of "Nature Poem about Flowers," Rohrer writes: "I thought this would be a terrible title for a poem, so I chose it and wanted to see if I could write a poem that somehow honored the title while veering far away from it. It turned into a poem about the clothes we wore in the nineties, but there are not-so-secret flowers throughout. I borrowed a line from Joshua Beckman too. For further information about demeaning jobs, see my book *The Others*."

MARGARET ROSS is the author of two books of poetry, *A Timeshare* (Omnidawn, 2015) and *Saturday* (The Song Cave, 2024). Her work has been recognized by a Wallace Stegner Fellowship and a Harper-Schmidt Fellowship. She is currently a visiting professor at the Iowa Writers' Workshop.

Ross writes: "'Cooperative' is based on stories I remember hearing growing up in New York City in the nineties. The architecture of an apartment building is something like a poem in stanzas: stacked rooms where lives play out and comedy and tragedy unfold side by side. One's floor is the other's ceiling."

Born in 1994 in the Chihuahuan Desert of Mexico, JAVIER SANDOVAL now teaches at the University of Alabama, where he has also served as poetry editor of *Black Warrior Review*. He has received Frontier Poetry's Global Poetry Prize and swamp pink's Indigenous Writers Award. His chapbook, *Blue Moon Looming* (CutBank Books, 2024), was named a Top Ten Debut by *Latino Stories*. Mostly, he loves to smoke on the stoop with his lady. You can follow him on Instagram for updates and jokes @JavierWantsCandy.

Sandoval writes: "I never expected 'Uncle Peyote' to become a poem. It started as a stand-up routine I wrote for a casino show in Seattle, but the pandemic put my comedy plans on hold. Back home in the South, I shifted my focus back to poetry and challenged myself to transform my best material into poems. This piece is one of my weirdest, so I'm especially proud to see it included in this anthology. It's a wonderful reminder that every part of life—and every attitude—can be turned into poetry.

"I also want to thank the editors at *Indiana Review*, Bernardo Wade and El Williams III, for originally publishing this piece. Not only was *Indiana Review* one of my first major publications, but both of these incredibly talented individuals continue to support my work to this day. Their dedication has set a standard I strive to meet in my own editorial work."

EMILY SCHULTEN was born in Bowling Green, Kentucky, in 1979. She is the author of three collections of poems, most recently *Easy Victims to the Charitable Deceptions of Nostalgia* (White Pine Press, 2024), winner of the 2023 White Pine Press Poetry Prize, and *The Way a Wound Becomes a Scar* (Kelsay Books, 2021). She is a 2024 Academy of American Poets Laureate Fellow and has received the 2024 Ralph Angel Poetry Prize, the 2023 Geri Digiorno Multi-Genre Prize, and the 2016 Erskine J. Poetry Prize. She is a professor and director of CFK Poetics at the College of the Florida Keys in Key West, Florida, where she is the current Poet Laureate.

Of "Nocturnal," Schulten writes: "We moved into our home just before we got pregnant—I'd tried for so long and in such trying ways to get pregnant—and this period of nesting was disrupted by the creatures we kept hearing wrestle and scratch and scrape overhead, a sound isolated to the space above where we slept. It was the pandemic, and James, the Orkin man, was the only person I saw regularly then. When he captured the pregnant rat, I saw the moment becoming a poem from where I stood in my driveway. (He estimated how many he'd caught by including a guess for the fetal litter size.) It was this place of discomfort in infestation I knew needed to be juxtaposed with the parallel discomfort of its elimination. There was so much vulnerability then, this stranger returning to the house again and again to find only traces and empty traps until he found a family, the delicacy of pregnancy, the quickness with which it can all be eliminated."

JANE SHORE was born in Newark in 1947 and grew up over her parents' dress store in North Bergen, New Jersey. She received the 1977 Juniper Prize and the 1986 Lamont Prize. *A Yes-or-No Answer* (Houghton Mifflin Harcourt, 2008) won the 2010 Poets' Prize. A Guggenheim Fellow, a Radcliffe Institute Fellow, and a Hodder Fellow at Princeton, she was awarded two NEA grants. *That Said: New and Selected Poems* was published by Houghton Mifflin Harcourt in 2012. She has taught at Harvard, Tufts, MIT, Sarah Lawrence, and the University of Washington, and was the Distinguished Poet-in-Residence at the University of Hawai'i at Manoa. Now a Professor of English Emerita, she taught at George Washington University in Washington, DC, for thirty-four years. "Who Knows One," the title poem of her new collection, was published in *The Best American Poetry 2019*, and "The Hat" was published in *The Best American Poetry 2024*. She lives in Vermont.

Of "I Am Sick of Reading Poems about Paintings by Vermeer," Shore writes: "Living and teaching for more than thirty years in Washington, DC, provided opportunities and experiences not available for me in rural Vermont. Highlights: the AIDS Quilt, the Million Mom March, Obama's first (bitterly cold) inauguration, and hundreds of poetry readings at the Folger and the Library of Congress. Also, the 1996 landmark Vermeer exhibition at the NGA, which I managed to go to twice, thanks to a dear friend who worked there, whose job it was to photograph (pre-show) all twenty-one Vermeer paintings! The exhibition endured two government shutdowns and a blizzard, but once inside the building, I was bombarded with Vermeer swag available for purchase at every turn. In the years following the show there appeared to be an upswing of *literary* swag as well. So why not hop on the Vermeer-poem-writing bandwagon too? This morning, I googled the NGA museum shop and found pages and pages of Vermeer merch, including *The Milkmaid* crew socks, a *View of Delft* mousepad, a *Woman in Blue Reading a Letter* sleeping mask, and a pair of *Girl with a Pearl Earring* pearl earrings in silver or gold. While I kvetch about being sick of reading Vermeer poems and the commodification of art, I managed to add one to the heap. On the NGA website, the show's simplified logo of *Girl with a Pearl Earring* sums it up perfectly: 'I survived the Vermeer Exhibition, National Gallery of Art 1995–1996,' her face as ubiquitous as Rosie the Riveter's."

MARTHA SILANO was born in New Brunswick, New Jersey, in 1961; she grew up in Metuchen, New Jersey. Thanks to Emily Dickinson and her second-grade teacher, Mrs. Everett, she became a poet at the age of seven. Her most recent books include *Terminal Surreal* (Acre Books, 2025), *Last Train to Paradise: New and Selected Poems* (Saturnalia Books, 2025), and *This One We Call Ours*, winner of the 2023 Blue Lynx Prize (Lynx House Press, 2024). She is also the author of *Gravity Assist* (2019), *Reckless Lovely* (2014), and *The Little Office of the Immaculate Conception* (2011), all published by Saturnalia Books. Her website is marthasilano.net.

Of "When I Learn Catastrophically," Silano writes: "In late November 2023, I was diagnosed with amyotrophic lateral sclerosis (ALS). Soon after finding out I had an incurable illness, I began to write poems about all this weird stuff going on with my body, along with what I was seeing, hearing, and feeling—mostly on walks, which soon became wheelchair rides, at a park near my home in Seattle, a place with old-growth cedars and Douglas firs, many native birds, and a stunning view of Mount Rainier. As for the idea to use an anagram generator to write a poem, the credit goes to poet Kelli Russell Agodon, who showed me how it's done. One day in early 2024, I started wondering what the anagrams of *amyotrophic lateral sclerosis* were. A few days later, I typed those three words into an anagram-generating website. Once I had a list of words, this poem pretty much wrote itself."

BRUCE SNIDER was born in Indiana in 1976. He is the author of three poetry collections, most recently *Fruit* (University of Wisconsin Press, 2020). Coeditor of *The Poem's Country: Place & Poetic Practice* (Pleiades Press, 2018), he lives in Baltimore and teaches in the Writing Seminars at Johns Hopkins University.

Snider writes: "I grew up in rural Indiana, in a house full of music by Hank Williams, Patsy Cline, Johnny Cash, Willie Nelson, and Dolly Parton. 'Trio' is from my next collection, *Blood Harmony*, which deals with, among other things, family, addiction, queerness, and country music."

MOSAB ABU TOHA is a Palestinian poet, short story writer, and essayist from Gaza. His first collection of poetry, *Things You May Find Hidden in My Ear* (City Lights, 2022), won the Palestine Book Award, the American Book Award, and the Derek Walcott Prize for Poetry. He founded the Edward Said Library in Gaza, which he hopes to rebuild. He recently won an Overseas Press Club Award for his "Letter from Gaza" columns for *The New Yorker*. His new book, *Forest of Noise* (Knopf, 2024), has been named a Notable Book of the Year by *The New York Times* and a *New Yorker* Essential Read.

TONY TOWLE was born in Manhattan in 1939, and has lived there most of his life, at present downtown, in Tribeca. He began writing poetry in 1960, when he was twenty-one, "out of the blue." A significant early event was taking poetry workshops with both Kenneth Koch and Frank O'Hara at the New School in the spring of 1963. His first major collection of poetry was *North*, the Frank O'Hara Award selection for 1970. In all, Towle has published thirteen collections of poetry, most recently *Noir* (2017), and two books of prose, *Memoir: 1960–1963*, an account of becoming a poet in New York, and his latest publication, *My First Three Books* (2020), combining an interview, photographs, and a CD of the poet reading early poems. From 1964 to 1981 Towle worked at Universal Limited Art Editions (ULAE), Tatyana Grosman's renowned print atelier in West Islip, Long Island. As Mrs. Grosman's secretary and administrative assistant, Towle had extensive informal contact with Barnett Newman, Jasper Johns, Helen Frankenthaler, Larry Rivers, Marisol, Robert Rauschenberg, Robert Motherwell, and Cy Twombly, among others. The experience of being around such prominent artists and their art was a unique and indelible experience.

Of "Birthdays," Towle writes: "It started with my daughter Rachel's birthday gift of the works of Fernando Pessoa, the great twentieth-century Portuguese poet, and she included a hefty biography about him as well. Pessoa was a poet I wanted to know about. Also, it is a fact I have been aware of for many decades that I had the same birthday as W. B. Yeats, June 13. In looking through Pessoa's biography, it jumped out at me that *he* had 'our' birthday too. I thought that this was a happenstance that should yield an interesting poem, but after several attempts, nothing worked, and I left the concept alone for a while.

From another angle, I have had, over many years, brief but priceless interactions with John Ashbery, which I remember clearly and exactly. When I read that Pessoa wrote to Yeats but didn't send the letter (and the book makes no mention of any knowledge of coincidental birthdays), I realized that it might be time to relate the Ashbery event that had an astrological theme (John is a Leo, by the way), that the unlikely chance of our meeting, and having the same astrologer, would work with the first, the 'preface' part of the poem. The resulting narration is all true, with no imaginative embellishments, including the astrological appraisal of myself at the end."

CINDY TRAN is the author of the poetry collection *Sonnet Crown for NYC* (2021), winner of the Thornwillow Patrons' Prize, and is the creator of a short film by the same name. She has received fellowships from NYSCA/NYFA, the Poetry Project, the Loft Literary Center, and Brooklyn Poets. Her work has been presented by the Shed, the BBC, Lincoln Center, and PBS.

Tran writes: "I woke up from a nap with the first two words of 'Blank Verse' and the rest poured out from decades of not knowing what to say."

DAVID TRINIDAD was born in Los Angeles in 1953. His numerous books include *New Playlist* (University of Pittsburgh Press, 2025), *Hollywood Cemetery* (Green Linden Press, 2025), *Sleeping with Bashō* (BlazeVOX [books], 2024), *Digging to Wonderland: Memory Pieces* (Turtle Point Press, 2022), and *Notes on a Past Life* (BlazeVOX, 2016). He is also the editor of *A Fast Life: The Collected Poems of Tim Dlugos* (Nightboat Books, 2011), *Punk Rock Is Cool for the End of the World: Poems and Notebooks of Ed Smith* (Turtle Point, 2019), and *Divining Poets: Dickinson*, an Emily Dickinson tarot deck (Turtle Point, 2019). Trinidad lives in Los Angeles.

Of "Never Argue with the Movies," Trinidad writes: "My ears always perk up when I hear a reference to poetry in old movies. This poem offers three examples of such references. I thought they give a pretty good idea of how general audiences feel about poetry: a lot of words that don't mean anything, something that's not worth reading, and 'an awful waste of broad shoulders.' The title is taken from Frank O'Hara's poem 'Fantasy.' Never argue with the movies? Of course one cannot live by such a dictum. *A Complete Unknown* being a recent case in point."

BERNARD WELT was born in Houston, Texas, and raised in Arlington, Virginia. He has published poetry as well as critical essays on the arts, especially cinema, some of which are collected in *Mythomania: Fantasies, Fables, and Sheer Lies in Contemporary American Popular Art* (Art Issues Press, 1996). He began his education in poetry at the Mass Transit open readings and the Folio Books readings in Washington, DC, and continued with an MA in writing from Johns Hopkins University and a PhD in literary studies from American University. He is the author of one collection of poems, *Serenade* (Z Press, 1979), has taught courses on dream studies and led dream-sharing groups for forty years, and is a contributing editor of *DreamTime*. He was a one-day champion on the quiz show *Jeopardy!* A professor emeritus at the Corcoran School of the Arts and Design at George Washington University, he will always be grateful to this anthology series for his introduction to many thoughtful readers, especially among high school students.

Welt writes: "'The Story So Far' is a friendly attack from within on autobiography, autofiction, and memoir. A huge amount of interest in selfhood just demonstrates that it's a troubled and maybe troubling concept, and maybe not enough satirical silliness has yet been attached to it. Who am I? What am I here for? I dunno; I just know the answers I get don't seem like enough. They may even seem bogus, or self-serving, or deeply tainted with ideology. I don't think I know who I am, in any really important sense, and I've already lived a long time. I hope it's OK to say that I feel a lot like Henry David Thoreau: 'I am a parcel of vain strivings tied / By a chance bond together.' Or John Ashbery: 'Am I myself, or a talking tree?'

"The advantage of poetry over prose is that you can let language lead the way into what you didn't know when you started to write, and prod you into accepting the possibility that seemingly random thoughts are as valid as the ones you cling to—as resonant, as useful, as productive, as true for you, at least in the moment. The stuff of poetry, the music of words and their evocation of images, is as wise as any ideas you might have, certainly any ideas you have about yourself. (OK, any ideas I've had about myself.) I think my work is play.

"I'd like to speak up for uncertainty, indeterminacy, and instability. People who reject every kind of nonmaterialist belief still betray the assumption that they have some essence, some destiny making them transcendently who they are. ('What do you think you'd have done if you lived in the sixteenth century?' 'Huh?!') They read history and politics and economics and somehow they still don't accept the fundamental reality of contingency. Maybe poetry can help. As thousands of people have said, probably some in this anthology series, I'd rather see poetry ask questions than insist on answers. If I might have been anyone, anywhere, I might work harder at understanding everyone everywhere with sympathy."

LESLEY WHEELER was born in New York in 1967. She is the author of six poetry collections, including *Mycocosmic* (Tupelo Press, 2025). Her other books include the hybrid memoir *Poetry's Possible Worlds* (Tinderbox Editions, 2022) and the novel *Unbecoming* (Aqueduct Press, 2020). She is poetry editor of *Shenandoah*.

Wheeler writes: "When 'Sex Talk' was accepted by *The Gettysburg Review*, I thought, 'Phew, glad to be in a print magazine for this one—fewer people will see it.' A mother's death is a terrible passage, but this poem, about the most awkward conversation I've ever had, could only have been written after I knew she would never again read my work. I'm grateful to editor Mark Drew for helping me find the right ending."

GEOFFREY YOUNG was born in Los Angeles in 1944. He has taught college classes in art and literature, and for twenty-seven years had his own contemporary art gallery in Great Barrington, Massachusetts, where he moved in 1982, after years in Berkeley. From 1975 to 2005 his small press, The Figures, published 135 books of poetry, fiction, and art criticism.

Of "The How and When of It," Young writes: "Kids find out about their own families as they perceive what is going on in other families. At twelve years old I was getting a sense of how things were in the neighborhood, but was caught by surprise to hear that my folks were getting divorced. The poem wanders its way to this narrative revelation after listening to Little Richard excite the air with his inimitable voice."

KEVIN YOUNG is the author of fifteen books of poetry and prose, including *Stones*; *Blue Laws: Selected & Uncollected Poems 1995–2015*; *Book of Hours*, winner of the Lenore Marshall Poetry Prize from the Academy of American Poets; *Jelly Roll: a blues*; *Bunk*; and *The Grey Album*. He is the poetry editor of *The New Yorker*. He is a member of the American Academy of Arts and Sciences, the American Academy of Arts and Letters, and the Society of American Historians. Named a chancellor of the Academy of American Poets in 2020, he lives and works in Washington, DC. He was the guest editor of *The Best American Poetry 2011*.

MAGAZINES WHERE THE POEMS WERE FIRST PUBLISHED

32 Poems, editor-in-chief George David Clark.
www.32poems.com

Action, Spectacle, publisher Adam Day.
www.action-spectacle.com

The Adroit Journal, editor-in-chief Peter LaBerge.
www.theadroitjournal.org

Alaska Quarterly Review, editor-in-chief Ronald Spatz.
www.aqreview.org

Allium, A Journal of Poetry & Prose, editor-in-chief Tony Trigilio.
www.allium.colum.edu

The American Poetry Review, editor-in-chief Elizabeth Scanlon.
www.aprweb.org

The American Scholar, poetry ed. Langdon Hammer.
www.theamericanscholar.org

The Best American Poetry Blog, ed. David Lehman.
blog.bestamericanpoetry.com

B O D Y, eds. Joshua Mensch, Christopher Crawford, Stephan Delbos, Michael Stein, and Jan Zikmund.
www.bodyliterature.com

The Brooklyn Rail, poetry ed. Erica Hunt.
www.brooklynrail.org

Bruiser, ed. Mark Wadley.
www.bruisermag.com

Chaudiere Books blog, ed. Rob McClennan.
www.chaudierebooks.blogspot.com

Copper Nickel, ed. Wayne Miller, poetry eds. Brian Barker and Nicky Beer.
www.copper-nickel.org

DMQ Review, editor-in-chief Sally Ashton.
www.dmqreview.com

Fence, poetry eds. Soham Patel, Max Winter, Patricia Killelea, Delicia Daniels, and Maxe Crandall.
www.fenceportal.org

Five Points, ed. Megan Sexton.
www.fivepoints.gsu.edu

FotoSpecchio, eds. Dan Murano and Grace Cavalieri.
www.fotospecchio.com

Gargoyle, ed. Richard Peabody.
www.gargoylemagazine.com

The Georgia Review, ed. Gerald Maa.
www.thegeorgiareview.com

Harvard Review, poetry ed. Major Jackson.
www.harvardreview.org

The Hopkins Review, editor-in-chief Dora Malech.
www.hopkinsreview.com

Indiana Review, poetry ed. Santi Valencia.
www.indianareview.iu.edu

Innisfree Poetry Journal, ed. Greg McBride.
www.innisfreepoetry.org

Julebord, eds. Elinor Nauen and Maureen Owen.
www.elinornauen.com/works.htm
www.maureenowen.com/books/julebord

The Kenyon Review, ed. Nicole Terez Dutton.
www.kenyonreview.org

Lana Turner, eds. Cal Bedient and David Lau.
www.lanaturnerjournal.com

Literary Imagination, ed. Archie Burnett.
www.academic.oup.com/litimag

Live Mag!, ed. Jeffrey Cyphers Wright.
www.livemag.org

The Massachusetts Review, poetry eds. Nathan McClain and Abigail Chabitnoy.
www.massreview.org

The Missouri Review, editor-in-chief Speer Morgan.
www.missourireview.com

The New York Review of Books, executive ed. Jana Prikryl.
www.nybooks.com

The New Yorker, poetry ed. Kevin Young.
www.newyorker.com

Orion, poetry ed. Camille T. Dungy.
www.orionmagazine.org

The Paris Review, poetry ed. Srikanth Reddy.
www.theparisreview.org

Ploughshares, poetry ed. John Skoyles.
www.pshares.org

Plume, editor-in-chief Daniel Lawless.
www.plumepoetry.com

Poetry, ed. Adrian Matejka.
www.poetryfoundation.org/poetrymagazine

Poetry Daily,
www.poets.com

Prairie Schooner, editor-in-chief Kwame Dawes.
www.prairieschooner.unl.edu

A Public Space, poetry ed. Brett Fletcher Lauer.
www.apublicspace.org

R&R, ed. Joseph Grantham.
www.relegationbooks.com/journal

Revel, editor-in-chief Peter Campion.
www.revel-literary.com

Smartish Pace, ed. Stephen Reichert.
www.smartishpace.com

The Southern Review, poetry ed. Jessica Faust.
www.thesouthernreview.org

The Threepenny Review, ed. Wendy Lesser.
www.threepennyreview.com

TriQuarterly, poetry ed. Daniel Fliegel.
www.triquarterly.org

Verse Daily, ed. J. P. Dancing Bear.
www.versedaily.org

The Yale Review, ed. Meghan O'Rourke.
www.yalereview.org

ACKNOWLEDGMENTS

The series editor wishes to thank Mark Bibbins for his many invaluable contributions. Warm thanks go also to Nin Andrews, Sally Ashton, Angela Ball, Denise Duhamel, Elaine Equi, Major Jackson, Stacey Lehman, Thomas Moody, and Mary Jo Salter; to Glen Hartley and Lynn Chu of Writers' Representatives; and to Kathy Belden, Daniel Cuddy, Kathryn Kenney-Peterson, and Ellie Crowley at Scribner. The poetry editors of the magazines that were our sources deserve applause; they are the secret heroes of contemporary poetry.

The series editor adds: "In 2024, Nan Graham announced her retirement as publisher of Scribner. Nan supervised *The Best American Poetry* from 1994 until 2020, and I will always cherish a remark she made that I overheard back in the late 1990s. Asked whether Scribner publishes poetry, she swiftly replied, 'Only the best,' a pun sweet to my ears. I thank her and all the hands-on editors I worked with since the inception of the series: John Glusman, Erika Goldman, Hamilton Cain, Gillian Blake, Alexis Gargagliano, Ashley Gilliam, and Kathy Belden. For the last twenty-six years, Mark Bibbins has, in his words, 'played Rudolph to your Santa,' a joke springing from our practice of sending letters of notification to poets around Christmastime; it has been a fruitful partnership.

"Publishing is a collaborative process, and there are more persons to acknowledge than space allows. My great thanks to all the guest editors with whom I have had the honor to work; they constitute, in A. E. Stallings's words, 'a who's who of US poetry elites.' It has been a special pleasure to collaborate with the art directors who have worked on *The Best American Poetry*. No effort toward a uniform cover design was made until 1995; we had facelifts again in 1999, 2005, and 2015. I had the great good fortune to choose the cover art year after year from the start."

Grateful acknowledgment is made of the magazines in which these poems first appeared and the magazine editors who selected them. A sincere attempt has been made to locate all copyright holders. Unless otherwise noted, copyright to the poems is held by the individual poets.

Gbenga Adesina, "The People's History of 1998," from *The Paris Review*. Reprinted by permission of the poet.

Hussain Ahmed, "Incantation for a Lake," from *A Public Space*. Reprinted by permission of the poet.

Indran Amirthanayagam, "At the Gate," from *The Best American Poetry Blog*. Reprinted by permission of the poet.

Margaret Atwood, "Tell Me Something Good." Copyright © 2024 O. W. Toad Ltd, first published in the collection *Paper Boat*, used by permission of CAA on behalf of O. W. Toad Ltd. Also appeared in *Orion*.

Catherine Barnett, "Nicholson Baker and I" from *Solutions for the Problem of Bodies in Space*. © 2024 by Catherine Barnett. Reprinted by permission of The Permissions Company, Inc., on behalf of Graywolf Press. Also appeared in *The Yale Review*.

David Beaudouin, "Annunciation," from *The Best American Poetry Blog*. Reprinted by permission of the poet.

Donald Berger, "Uncle Sadness," from *R&R*. Reprinted by permission of the poet.

Camille Carter, "Thoughts about Inheritance," from *Five Points*. Reprinted by permission of the poet.

Grace Cavalieri, "White Suit," from *FotoSpecchio*. Reprinted by permission of the poet.

Christopher Chambers, "What About This," from *Fence*. Reprinted by permission of the poet.

Dorothy Chan, "Triple Sonnet for Nomi Malone," from *The American Poetry Review*. Reprinted by permission of the poet.

Heather Christle, "Aubade," from *The Southern Review*. Reprinted by permission of the poet.

Lor Clincy, "Wishes for Black Women," from *Allium, A Journal of Poetry & Prose*. Reprinted by permission of the poet.

Andrea Cohen, "Fable," from *Poetry*. Reprinted by permission of the poet.

Billy Collins, "Thought a Rarity on Paper," from *Water, Water*. © 2024 by Billy Collins. Reprinted by permission of Penguin Random House. Also appeared in *The New Yorker*.

Katie Condon, "Book Blurb in the American Style," from *Copper Nickel*. Reprinted by permission of the poet.

Morri Creech, "A Letter from Rome," from *The Hopkins Review*. Reprinted by permission of the poet.

Patricia Davis-Muffett, "Climate Anxiety," from *Smartish Pace*. Reprinted by permission of the poet.

Armen Davoudian, "The Ring," from *The Palace of Forty Pillars*. © 2024 by Armen Davoudian. Reprinted by permission of Tin House Books. Also appeared in *The Hopkins Review*.

Greg Delanty, "To Our Indolent Cancer," from *The New York Review of Books*. Reprinted by permission of the poet.

Abigail Dembo, "The Travelers," from *Five Points*. Reprinted by permission of the poet.

Jose Hernandez Diaz, "My Kafka Prose Poem," from *Portrait of the Artist as a Brown Man*. © 2025 by Jose Hernandez Diaz. Reprinted by permission of The Permissions Company, Inc., on behalf of Red Hen Press. Also appeared in *The Southern Review*.

Tishani Doshi, "Egrets, While War," from *Harvard Review*. Reprinted by permission of the poet.

Denise Duhamel, "Poem in Which This Fathead 'Fat Ass' Admits It," from *DMQ Review*. Reprinted by permission of the poet.

Elaine Equi, "Lorca's Guitar," from *Action, Spectacle*. Reprinted by permission of the poet.

Gerald Fleming, "Two Thousand," from *B O D Y*. Reprinted by permission of the poet.

Joanna Fuhrman, "How to Change the Filter on the Developing Cell Matter in Your Womb," from *Data Mind*. Copyright © 2025 by Northwestern University. Published 2025 by Curbstone Books / Northwestern University Press. All rights reserved. Also appeared in *The Georgia Review*.

Amy Gerstler, "Postcard," from *Revel*. Reprinted by permission of the poet.

James Allen Hall, "Inheritance at Corresponding Periods of Life, at Corresponding Seasons of the Year, as Limited by Sex," from *The Adroit Journal*. Reprinted by permission of the poet. The poem also appeared on *Poetry Daily*.

Jeffrey Harrison, "Amnesia," from *The Threepenny Review*. Reprinted by permission of the poet.

Robert Hass, "A Sunset," from *The New Yorker*. Reprinted by permission of the poet.

Bob Hicok, "The call to worship," from *The New Yorker*. Reprinted by permission of the poet.

Nazifa Islam, "The Wind Whipped Tears into My Eyes," from *The Southern Review*. Reprinted by permission of the poet. The poem also appeared on *Verse Daily*.

Henry Israeli, "Escape Artists," from *The Massachusetts Review*. Reprinted by permission of the poet.

Fatima Jafar, "In the End of the Beginning of Our Lives," from *The Kenyon Review*. Reprinted by permission of the poet.

Brionne Janae, "The Heart," from *Allium, A Journal of Poetry & Prose*. Reprinted by permission of the poet.

Raphael Jenkins, "Two men too man to mourn," from *Indiana Review*. Reprinted by permission of the poet.

Virginia Konchan, "Miraculous," from *The Missouri Review*. Reprinted by permission of the poet.

Victoria Kornick, "Eileen," from *Copper Nickel*. Reprinted by permission of the poet.

Marianne Kunkel, "Apostate Abecedarian," from *The Threepenny Review*. Reprinted by permission of the poet.

Michael Lally, "DC 1972," from *R&R*. Reprinted by permission of the poet.

Danusha Laméris, "Second Sight," from *The Adroit Journal*. Reprinted by permission of the poet.

Hailey Leithauser, "Five Postcards," from *Innisfree Poetry Journal* and *32 Poems*. Reprinted by permission of the poet.

Amit Majmudar, "Patronage," from *32 Poems*. Reprinted by permission of the poet.

Chris Mason, "Well Water," from *Bruiser*. Reprinted by permission of the poet.

Greg McBride, "Know Thyself," from *FotoSpecchio*. Reprinted by permission of the poet.

Jill McDonough, "What We Are For," from *The Threepenny Review*. Reprinted by permission of the poet.

Joyelle McSweeney, "Death Styles 5/6/2021: *Terminator 2*, Late Style," from *Death Styles*. © 2024 by Joyelle McSweeney. Reprinted by permission of The Permissions Company, Inc., on behalf of Nightboat Books. Also appeared in *Lana Turner*.

Ange Mlinko, "The Bougainvillea Line," from *The American Scholar*. Reprinted by permission of the poet.

Nicholas Montemarano, "A Neighborly Day in This Beautywood," from *Copper Nickel*. Reprinted by permission of the poet.

Yehoshua November, "What About the Here and Now?" from *The Concealment of Endless Light*. © 2024 by Yehoshua November. Reprinted by permission of Orison Books, Inc. All rights reserved. Also appeared in *TriQuarterly*.

Sharon Olds, "Health-Food Panties," from *Prairie Schooner*. Reprinted by permission of the poet.

Michael Ondaatje, "November," from *A Year of Last Things*. © 2024 by Michael Ondaatje. Reprinted by permission of Alfred A. Knopf. Also appeared in *The Threepenny Review*.

Pádraig Ó Tuama, "Do You Believe in God?" from *Kitchen Hymns*. © 2025 by Pádraig Ó Tuama. Reprinted by permission of The Permissions Company, Inc., on behalf of Copper Canyon Press. Also appeared in *Alaska Quarterly Review*.

Jose Padua, "Godzilla Meets the Beast," from *The Brooklyn Rail*. Reprinted by permission of the poet.

Elise Paschen, "After *Killers of the Flower Moon*," from *Blood Wolf Moon*. © 2025 by Elise Paschen. Reprinted by permission of The Permissions Company, Inc., on behalf of Red Hen Press. Also appeared in *Poetry*.

Alison Pelegrin, "Zero Bothers Given," from *The Southern Review*. Reprinted by permission of the poet.

Donald Platt, "Streak," from *Plume*. Reprinted by permission of the poet.

Jana Prikryl, "The Channel," from *The Paris Review*. Reprinted by permission of the poet.

Elizabeth Robinson, "The Extinct World," from *Lana Turner*. Reprinted by permission of the poet.

Matthew Rohrer, "Nature Poem about Flowers," from *Army of Giants*. © 2024 by Matthew Rohrer. Reprinted by permission of The Permissions Company, Inc., on behalf of Wave Books. Also appeared in *The American Poetry Review*.

Margaret Ross, "Cooperative," from *The Paris Review*. Reprinted by permission of the poet.

Javier Sandoval, "Uncle Peyote," from *Indiana Review*. Reprinted by permission of the poet.

Emily Schulten, "Nocturnal," from *Ploughshares*. Reprinted by permission of the poet.

Jane Shore, "I Am Sick of Reading Poems about Paintings by Vermeer," from *Literary Imagination*. Reprinted by permission of the poet.

Martha Silano, "When I Learn Catastrophically," from *The Missouri Review*. Reprinted by permission of the poet.

Bruce Snider, "Trio," from *The Georgia Review*. Reprinted by permission of the poet.

Mosab Abu Toha, "Two Watches," from *Forest of Noise*. © 2024 by Mosab Abu Toha. Reprinted by permission of Alfred A. Knopf. Also appeared in *Ploughshares*.

Tony Towle, "Birthdays," from *Julebord*. Reprinted by permission of the poet. The poem also appeared on *The Best American Poetry Blog*.

Cindy Tran, "Blank Verse," from *The Southern Review*. Reprinted by permission of the poet.

David Trinidad, "Never Argue with the Movies," from *R&R*. Reprinted by permission of the poet.

Bernard Welt, "The Story So Far," from *Gargoyle*. Reprinted by permission of the poet.

Lesley Wheeler, "Sex Talk," from *The Gettysburg Review*. Reprinted by permission of the poet. The poem also appeared on *Poetry Daily*.

Geoffrey Young, "The How and When of It," from *Live Mag!* and the Chaudiere Books blog. Reprinted by permission of the poet.

Kevin Young, "Snapdragon," from *The American Poetry Review*. Reprinted by permission of the poet.